S0-BRN-469

THE 6,000 BEARDS
OF ATHOS

THE 6,000 BEARDS
OF ATHOS

RALPH H. BREWSTER

Introduction by Jonathan Keates

MICHAEL RUSSELL

Text and illustrations © Harry Brewster
Introduction © Jonathan Keates 1999
First published 1935

This edition published 1999
by Michael Russell (Publishing) Ltd
Wilby Hall, Wilby, Norwich NR16 2JP

Typeset in Sabon by The Typesetting Bureau
Allen House, East Borough, Wimborne, Dorset
Printed and bound in Great Britain
by Biddles Ltd, Guildford and King's Lynn

All rights reserved
ISBN 0 85955 251 9

Contents

Introduction

One of the most familiar experiences for readers of travel books is that they end up knowing more about the personality of the traveller than about the place he or she has visited. The vogue for travel writing which became one of the dominant trends of the 1980s, spawning dozens of smart magazines (most of them fairly short-lived, as things turned out) and generating lavish supplements in the leisure sections of broadsheet newspapers, depended for its continuance on our sense of the traveller as star protagonist rather than guide or informant. A new and entirely shameless species of egoism moved the wanderer from his discreet position at one side of the picture, appropriately dwarfed by surrounding mountains, icebergs or water-falls, to a dominant centre stage, in which alien environments were there, it seemed, merely to enhance his attractiveness to envious and admiring readers.

In fact this idea of the voyager as itinerant ego was hardly new. Earlier writers, however, had blended more effectively with the people and places they visited and been altogether less blasé about reacting to what they saw with straightforward interest and surprise. *The 6,000 Beards of Athos*, as the mocking oddity of its title suggests, is hardly a conventional account of a trip to the Holy Mountain of Greek Orthodoxy, but the controlling vision of its author engages us with a kind of vulnerable eccentricity which provides a fascinating counterweight to the noisily opinionated posturing of today's travel writers.

Orthodoxy of whatever variety seems to have been anathema to Ralph Brewster. He was himself something of an exotic, the child of one of those expatriate families – in this case a mixture of American and German – who created a species of cultural aristocracy in Florence during the late nineteenth and early twentieth centuries. Sent to finish his education at King's College, Cambridge during the late 1920s, he became bored with undergraduate life, and set off to Greece to join an archaeological dig in Corinth. The experience turned out to be less immediately thrilling than promised. A lowly assignment piecing together newly uncovered potsherds was enough to make him want to return, if not at once to King's, then to something a shade more glamorous, and he spent some time working in a Berlin film studio before Cambridge indulgently welcomed him back again.

The university's faith in Brewster's promise is significant. A gifted linguist, he was also an exceptionally talented musician (his parents' villa at the foot of Bellosguardo had welcomed Liszt and Brahms, and Ethel Smyth had been a family friend). Thoughts were entertained for a time of becoming a conductor, and musical passions inspired him a decade or so later, while living in Vienna, to found an international magazine entitled *World Music*.

It was perhaps the only project on which he was seriously keen to persevere. The notion of Ralph 'settling down' to anything is implausible, not just because his footloose, amoral charm provided a suitable context, as it were, for his homosexuality, an aspect of life which, if not dealt with directly in his published writings, is glanced at among their pages with an unembarrassed nonchalance surprising in the literature of the period.

The age itself was in any case one of transience and anticipation. With an inevitable hindsight we look back on the inter-war years as an epoch of fevered restlessness in which a sense of waiting for something to happen was matched at the end by ironies whose satisfying grimness attained unimaginable proportions.

Glib as such a view may be, *The 6,000 Beards of Athos* seems archetypally a book for its times, frivolous and iconoclastic perhaps, but entirely true to the nature of the world which produced it. We need to remember, what's more, that Greece itself was a byword, at the time, for extreme political volatility. Born out of independence struggles with the Ottoman Empire, the nation had signally failed to reconcile attempts at creating a modern parliamentary democracy with ancient traditions of family feuding, deference to local bosses and the writing of laws in blood rather than ink. During the 1920s and 1930s the Greek monarchy had toppled on several occasions only to be restored. We can understand the shocked reaction of a foreign diplomat on being told by some Athenian children that they enjoyed school, 'because we get so many holidays, one for every time His Majesty goes into exile and one for every time he gets his throne back'.

To successive upheavals, however, Mount Athos remained indifferent, epitomising the *vita contemplativa* on its peninsula in what had until very recently been a south-western department of the Turkish Sultan's domain. The cluster of monasteries, with their wonderworking icons and their Byzantine libraries, had always fascinated travellers to the Levant, and since the beginning of the nineteen century the place had become an embodiment, inevitably somewhat romanticised, of tenacious Christian survival amid what Europeans liked to consider the barbarous overlordship of Muslim pashas, beys and aghas. Between Robert Curzon, who visited Athos in 1837 on the track of Greek manuscripts (which he was none too scrupulous in snapping up during his travels among Levantine monasteries), and Robert Byron (more famous for his Persian wanderings as a pert young undergraduate in *The Road to Oxiana*), who distilled the Athos experience in his underwhelmingly-entitled book *The Station*, the Holy Mountain proved irresistible to travellers in search of something to offset the encroaching vulgarities of mass tourism elsewhere in the Mediterranean.

Neither politics nor religion seem much to have interested the twenty-nine-year-old Ralph Brewster, and he himself is a trifle vague, in his opening pages, as to what at first drew him to Athos. Since he was eminently someone whose gift was for embracing the pleasures and possibilities of the immediate moment, we have no reason to doubt his implication that sheer curiosity and nothing else spurred him to set off with his cameras (in addition to all his other talents he was an expert photographer) from Thessaloniki for an extended tour of the various monasteries.

He was not going alone. This quixotic adventure required a Sancho Panza, and Iorgos, versatile, experienced, streetwise and significantly youthful and good-looking – 'not at all typically Greek but more like an Arab beauty from Africa' – perfectly fitted the bill. Given what is suggested as to the frustrations of a society in which everything female, even a hen or a cow, is banned, and given also the indiscriminate sexuality of the old Ottoman Levant, so outrageous yet so alluring to western Europeans, the presence of a handsome foreign wanderer and his decidedly personable body-servant was clearly unnerving to the monks and hermits, and its various effects provide an amusing subtext to Brewster's narrative.

Those whose concept of Greek Orthodoxy is one of awe and mystery, a *mise-en-scène* of tall-hatted archimandrites, flickering tapers,

Byzantine chanting from the shadows beyond the iconostasis, and the Pantokrator with his crooked finger gazing in eternal compassion from the gold-ground mosaic of an apsidal conch, may be somewhat taken aback by *The 6,000 Beards of Athos*. Though not deliberately irreverent, Brewster approaches his theme with absolute candour and realism, matching these with a prose style of disarming simplicity. Without trying to debunk the holiness of Athos, he reveals instead its intrinsically human side by recording the stories and words of the monks themselves, won over as they so easily were by his invincible charm. Tales like those of the porter at Philotheou, with hair-raising memories of the freezing Klondyke, or the happier story of Panos the deacon at Kafsokalyvia, enhance rather than detract from the enduring image of Athos through their emphasis on worldliness as a vital spur in the quest for spiritual inspiration.

It has to be said, nevertheless, that Brewster's attitude towards the entire phenomenon of the Holy Mountain and its monasteries, whether coenobian or idiorhythmic (a distinction explained in the mini-glossary), remains one of mischievous amusement. We might almost suppose that he had deliberately selected Iorgos for the boy's power to distract the brothers from their meditations, especially if the equivocal episode at the close of chapter 10 is anything to go by. *The 6,000 Beards* ends as abruptly as it began, and we are treated to some voluminous appendices, including the extraordinary assessment of each monastery on the bases of 'food', 'rooms', 'bugs', and 'WC'. The lavatory at Esphigmenou is deemed worth visiting for the sake of its architecture, Koutloumoussiou swarms with vermin, Diochiariou's food is 'disgusting; worst on Athos' and Lavras's rooms are sunk under 'Turkish gloom'.

We are not told what happened to Iorgos, though we should like to know. As for Ralph Brewster, his bizarre adventures during the Second World War as a stateless bohemian trapped in Hungary before escaping to Italy are memorably recounted in his buoyant memoir *Wrong Passport* (1952). From Milan, where he had lived in disguise as an astrologer, he managed to get home to his family's villa at San Francesco in Florence, narrowly avoiding execution on the way by some drunken American soldiers in the Apennines. Only a few years later, with the *World Music* project successfully launched, he died in Florence of a sudden heart attack. Was he therefore a classic case of unfulfilled promise? I think not. His books, imbued with a restless, wide-ranging curiosity, speak for him, the work of a man whose constant question about those he came across was 'Yes, but is he *interesting*?'

JONATHAN KEATES

I

Prologue

'But of course there are women on Mount Athos! How would it be possible for six thousand men to live together without a single woman? I visited the monastery of Lavra last year, and I am sure that the under-secretary, at any rate, is a woman disguised as a monk. I make a photograph of him: there can hardly be any doubt. You have only to look at his face – her face.'

This statement, made by the Italian archaeologist, Dr L–, was for me the final touch. I could restrain my curiosity about the Holy Mountain no longer. I felt I must go there and penetrate its mystery.

Were there women on Mount Athos? Or was this only the imagination of an Italian to whom the idea of a land without women was a natural impossibility? At any rate, this had not been suggested to me before. But then everything I heard about Athos was so contradictory. No two people who spoke to me about it ever said the same thing. I knew, of course, the ordinary facts: that it was a peninsula, isolated from the world, twelve hours in a steamer from Salonica; that it had existed for a thousand years as a virtually independent republic of monks; and that from the start its laws had forbidden admittance not only to women, but also to eunuchs, beardless persons and even female animals. But it was impossible to get a definite impression of what life was like in this strange world of monks and hermits.

Some people had told me of the extraordinary poetry of life in the ancient monasteries, each of which had a special character of its own, and where nothing had changed since the days of the Byzantine Empire. Some spoke of the fantastic landscape and vegetation; others of the hermits living in caves in the rocks of a marble mountain, 6,000 feet high, and practising incredible asceticism, like the early Egyptian Fathers. I heard of anchorites who flagellated themselves, and spent their lives with chains on their arms and legs. A young Frenchman, whom I had met once in Athens, described a visit he and a friend had made in the winter, when there was deep snow, and how charming the monks had been, looking after them and lighting great fires for them in their rooms. And another Frenchman, who had been one of the chief officers at Salonica during the war, told me a series of scandalous stories, how the monks went off to a little brothel-town just across the frontier of the Mountain, where it joined the mainland of Macedonia, and how there was a tower at the principal port, where foundlings were brought and deposited, later to be brought up as monks. He described, too, the enormous wealth of the Russian monks (every Orthodox country has monks on Athos) before the war, under the Empire of the Czars. Every monk, he said, had an income of Frs. 70,000, so they didn't know what to do with the money. They took to strange hobbies: one started a collection of telescopes and optical instruments, continually acquiring new ones, which he collected as if they were rare bits of china and consequently never made any proper use of.

I did not know what to believe. But it was the remark of Dr L–, made casually at a party, that caused me finally to make up my mind. I felt I must see the Holy Mountain for myself and learn the truth about this medieval society.

A month later I was in Athens, equipped with cameras and photographic materials. A couple of friends were to have met me there and accompanied me to the Holy Mountain, but at the last moment they were prevented from coming. It was necessary, however, to have someone to help me with my photographic tackle. Whom should I take? I decided it would be best to get hold of a Greek, who being of the same race as the majority of the monks, would be most use on the spot – and more likely to help me to solve these problems than a foreigner. Even though I myself speak modern Greek well, it would be rather a handicap to be accompanied by another foreigner. There would be a danger of my being regarded as an ordinary tourist, and of receiving only a superficial impression of the life of the monks.

I inquired through friends about a general factotum. Various people were suggested to me, but they either failed to inspire confidence, or were so insufferably dull that the prospect of being continually with them for six or eight weeks was unthinkable. Then I met Iorgos, who was particularly recommended to me. He did not look at all typically Greek, but more like an Arab beauty from Africa.

Iorgos was only twenty-one, but had had a very crowded life. He had been a singer, a dancer, an actor, and as such had toured all the Greek provinces. He had worked in a newspaper office, also in a tailor's shop, and had just finished his military service as a sailor. He could do anything – from cooking a superb dinner to mending clothes, and had a thoroughly developed oriental talent for bargaining.

He was very cheerful, always full of jokes and amusing stories. Everybody liked him, and indeed everybody seemed to know him. Cabinet ministers greeted him in the streets, and he was recognised and welcomed in the slums. He had, of course, no culture, and no particular schooling, but nevertheless took an interest in Shakespeare, Tolstoi and Michelangelo, and continually asked me intelligent questions about them.

Iorgos's keenest interest was perhaps the stage. He found the life picturesque and fascinating, but he considered it impossible to make a decent living by acting in Greece. His relations wished him to become a policeman – but he wanted to travel, and was thinking of finding a job as a wireless operator on some large ship, which would enable him to see the world. When I proposed visiting Mount Athos, he was thrilled at the idea, and I congratulated myself at having found someone with whom I should not be bored.

After laying in a stock of provisions, we took the steamer to Salonica, accompanied by a dog called Nera, who was on her annual visit to the North for the hunting season and to get puppies. The trip lasted two nights and a day, quite a voyage. And as we travelled 'deck', which in Greece is always far more amusing than to go first class – at least when the weather is fine – the fare was only 5s. 6d. per head.

It was a very spirited journey, and there was plenty of time to make acquaintances. We spread our pneumatic rubber mattresses on the deck, which made more comfortable beds than if we had been in a first-class cabin. Everybody came and touched them, quite thrilled to see how soft they were. In the morning Iorgos made breakfast on a spirit lamp, with hot chocolate, egg-and-anchovy sandwiches, salted almonds and fresh fruit. The sea was calm, the sun warm, and the whole world seemed jolly. The landscape changed continually. Every now and then we put in at some little port, and we remained several hours at Volo, in a magnificent gulf, with Mount Pelion and its numerous villages glittering in the sun.

The people on board told jokes and stories; a half-wit sang songs. A group of sailors, going home on leave to Salonica, danced together most of the night.

Finally, we arrived at the great port of Salonica. The town has a far more Eastern character than Athens, and we were at once plunged into the swirl of oriental life, where Iorgos showed himself perfectly at home. We were met at the harbour by the keeper of a small coffee-and-jam shop, who came to fetch the dog. We had very little money with us (more was being sent on), and did not know where to leave our luggage – twelve pieces in all, consisting of rubber mattresses, picnic baskets, a tent, mosquito nets, etc., etc. The jam-shop keeper, however, put them in his back shop, while we went off to look for rooms. But the Salonica Exhibition was on; the town was packed. We tried fourteen hotels: not a room to be had, only single beds in dormitories overrun with bugs.

Then an idea occurred to Iorgos. A friend of his would put us up, a married Greek woman, of whom he had seen a good deal in Athens a few months before, when she had gone there to have a baby (from a lover). We visited her. She had three charming children and a husband in America. But she could not take us in, as her husband was suspicious and was having her watched. It would not do for two young men to spend the night in her house. So she gave us coffee instead, and insisted on Iorgos reading her fortune in the dregs, as he had done for her before in Athens.

We wandered on in the violet dusk through the streets of the town, crowded with men of every nationality and race, Jews, Italians, Spaniards, Turks, and Macedonians. Street vendors were shouting on all sides. Finally, we went back to the coffee-and-jam shop, but the owner was unable to help us. There was no ship sailing for Athos till the following evening. It was necessary to spend the night somewhere, and by now it was getting late. The only thing to do seemed to be to sleep in the tent, but it was miles to get out of town, and the maze of narrow dark streets in the old part of the town was unknown to us.

Then, passing a variety theatre, near the big 'White Tower' on the waterfront, Iorgos met an elderly man, a theatre manager, who appeared delighted to see him. We explained our dilemma. The manager said he had a room, but could only take one person. Would Iorgos come to share his room with him? he asked. But Iorgos didn't want to.

'You know what he wants,' he whispered to me. But the manager seemed eager, and walked off with Iorgos to a dark corner and offered to give him an engagement in his company if he would spend the night with him.

'But I don't want an engagement just now; I'm just going to Mount Athos,' said Iorgos.

The manager was dumbfounded.

'What on earth are you going to that God-forsaken place for?' he asked.

We left him and walked off in the darkness along the quay – dead tired. We didn't know what to do or where to go. Suddenly a man came towards us out of the night.

'Well, I'm damned it that isn't Adriana,' cried Iorgos. The two greeted each other. It was years since they had met. Adriana was an impersonator, and had an engagement in Salonica as 'Josephine Baker'.

'Come along with me,' he said. 'I'll find you a room for the night.' And we walked off light-heartedly, Adriana speaking all the way of his recent successes in Egypt and his adventures there.

He took us to the house where he was staying on the water-front, looking out across the lights of the port, with the clear stars above, and at last we found somewhere to stay. In the rooms round about were other members of the theatrical company and strange sounds came from all sides, shrill voices, the shaking of beds, snatches of arias. But we were too tired to be affected by noise of any kind, or by the hardness of the beds. In five minutes we were asleep.

Next morning Iorgos left for Mount Athos with part of our luggage, taking the land route as he wished to visit friends on the way. And in the evening I took the steamer for Athos, travelling 'deck'.

But this was a journey of a very different kind to that between Athens and Salonica; the steamer was very small and crammed. The night was cold and a strong wind blew through the rigging. It was impossible to find protection anywhere.

It was a clear night with a full moon, but there was a strange gloom about the steamer. Something of the mystery of the Mountain towards which we were steaming seemed to hang over the ship. A herd of black he-goats were crowded in a corner, and there were a number of peasants dressed in black, who sat without moving, uttering only occasional remarks. They were in the charge of monks who were bringing them to their monasteries. One or two more important monks moved about smiling on all sides before retiring to their cabins.

I sat on a bench, enveloped in the oily smell of the engines, and felt that I was making a journey backwards in time, into an unknown century. Towards daybreak the atmosphere became less sinister. It was damp and cold. There were no signs of any movement. A few figures, some in the black dress of monks, lay sleeping, huddled in corners, or in the shelter of coils of rope. The black he-goats bleated sadly; every now and then one tried to make more room for himself, and began to butt his neighbour.

The little steamer had now passed round the southern point of the peninsula of Longos, which is the central finger of the three promontories called the Chalcidice, and was heading for the eastern one, the whole of which bears the name Mount Athos, or 'The Holy Mountain'. The steamer throbbed softly; the dark heavy water broke on its bows, slipped past the hull, and spread a trail of grey bubbles behind the ship on the mirror of the sea. Gradually the lonely yellow lamp at the masthead began to pale; the stars became fewer. A cold luminous green came into the sky behind the long line of land ahead. In the half light we seemed to be making for the centre of an immense cliff some twenty miles long, lower on the left, where it adjoined the mainland. On the right it rose in a tremendous pyramid 6,000 feet high, tumbling directly into the sea. For nearly an hour I watched the coming of day. The land took on form, showing its green covering of forest and its rocky coastline, with here and there the white mass of a monastery standing out against the dark background. The sea grew opalescent. But the bare white stone mountain was still mysterious with deep blue shadows, its edge touched by the beams of the invisible sun. The ship came to life. It was approaching a little port lying in the shadow at the water's edge. There were only a few building: above one of them was a small church reached by a staircase, with a flat Byzantine dome on a small drum. A stream joined the sea beside a mill, some boats with monks at the oars came towards us. The steamer cast anchor.

I was at Daphni, the port of Athos, the oldest republic in the world. This was the goal of my journey.

2

Karyes

After satisfying the policemen that I was not a woman disguised, and showing my passport, I was allowed to land. I breakfasted at one of the two little inns on the quay, while mules were being found to take my luggage up to the little town of Karyes, the capital of the Holy Mountain, high on the other (eastern) slope of the peninsula. Every visitor to Athos must, as his first step, present his letter of introduction to the Holy Synod in Karyes, before being able to visit the monasteries.

There are, of course, no roads on Athos, no wheeled vehicles. The paths are rough and stony, with wide steps where it is steep. One must go everywhere on foot or by mule. Each monastery provides animals free of charge for the traveller to continue his journey to the next. It was a steep climb of over two hours to the summit, the path winding among the rocks and shrubs and through belts of trees, chestnuts, planes and wild oaks, mostly rather small. A traveller of the last century called Athos the 'original home of the chestnut', as he had never encountered them anywhere else so old and so luxuriating. But, unfortunately, the financial losses of late years have compelled the monasteries to sell their trees, and there are only a few places left – for example, near the monasteries of Chilandari and Lavra – where there are tracts of chestnuts to be seen in their former magnificence.

The herbs by the wayside smelt sweetly as I climbed the steep track. Occasionally, I passed a monk seated placidly sideways on a mule. At last, when it was nearly noon, I reached the top of the ridge. The sun was blazing; crickets and cicadas sang on every side. I drank from a fountain in a circle of elms, one of the many delicious springs to be found in all parts of Athos. Through the trees I saw not far away the roofs of Karyes surrounded by outlying villas and gardens. To the left was a great mass of white building surmounted by spires and green-topped cupolas, the 'Serail', a Russian skite. This eastern slope, however, was quite different in character from the one I had just climbed. It was a smiling landscape running gently from the sea two or three miles away, covered with vineyards and fields of silvery olives like those of Tuscany. To the right the peak of Mount Athos rose pale and white in the midday glare from its forest-covered buttresses.

In 1679 a book was published in London called *The Present State of the Greek and Armenian Churches*, by P. Rycaut. It contains a description of Karyes:

> The Town of Kareis, or Kareais, as they write it, is seated about the middle of the Mountain, where a plentiful Market is held every Saturday, to which great numbers of people (I mean the Male Sex) do there meet, where the Fryars buy cheese, and eggs, and as many male Sheep and Goats, as may supply them with sufficient provision of Wooll for working. Here also they sell their Manufactories, such as iron worked into Shovels, Tongs, Horseshoes, etc, also Boots, Shoes, Beads, Crosses, and what else is the fruit of their Lands, or Surplusage of their provisions, for all which they are paid in ready money.
>
> At this place the chief Monasteries have a house or lodging to receive their respective members who have occasions at that place. . . .
>
> There is near adjoyning a very fair Church, built by Constantine the Great, dedicated to the Assumption of the Blessed Virgin, which they call the 'sleeping of the blessed Virgin', which church being very ancient, was repaired about 164 years past, as appears by an inscription on one of the Walls.
>
> For mantainance of these publick Buildings and the persons which inhabit them, and for defraying the charges of Candles, Oyl and Lamps, and supporting those who Weekly (that is on Market-days) read the Liturgy, every monastery is taxed in proportion to its Revenue.

The conservatism of Mount Athos is such that hardly a line of Rycaut's description requires to be altered to suit present-day conditions. Weaving is no longer carried on to any extent on the Mountain, and stuffs for clothes are imported from England. But the actual tailoring of garments is done by monks.

Karyes has only one main street, about 250 yards long, winding round in a curve. Many short, narrow streets branch off on each side, to lose themselves after a little among the fields. The town has a quite special character of its own, in complete contrast to most small towns in Greece or on the Islands. It has none of their gaiety and brightness. The houses instead are far more northern in character, with projecting upper stories after the Turkish manner. And they are painted not white, but a cold, blue grey.

The ancient church of the Protáton is off the main street, approached through an arched way in the base of the eighteenth-century bell-tower. In another tower nearby, which is far older, are preserved the archives of the Holy Mountain.

Along the principal street are the shops, two diminutive cafés for the peasants and mule-drivers, and, at the far end, the inn. It is kept by a layman, but must observe fasts in the same way as a monastery. Most of the shops are shoemakers' and tailors', or general stores. In these one finds candles, soap, pans, paper, rosaries and wooden spoons made by the monks, and even eggs, usually imported. In one little shop I found rows and rows of bottles containing oils and unguents distilled from trees and herbs. The dark green oil from laurel leaves is the fashionable hair preparation: it certainly appears to be highly efficacious. Other oils are designed as remedies for ills in almost every conceivable part of the body.

They have a strange atmosphere, these little narrow streets, where the sun scarcely penetrates. They are very neat, very quiet; uncomfortably quiet, perhaps. There is no harsh sound, no abrupt movement. Everything is as it were muffled. A mule is led through the street to a fountain: to ride it would be disrespectful. A black-robed monk glides silently past, or comes and stands at the door of a shop. There is no sound of conversation, no laughter. At Karyes silence is a force which descends on any sound that would make itself heard, and smothers it like a blanket.

And it is a town without a woman or a child. Nowhere else on the Holy Mountain is one so struck by their absence as here. During a thousand years no woman has given birth; no children have played their games in the streets. For a thousand years Karyes has preserved its solemn calm.

But Karyes is not only a town of monks. It is also the metropolis and centre of government of a country of 7,000 inhabitants. There is a Greek Governor living in a villa outside; his work, however, is mainly nominal. The tiny police force too have little to occupy them. Internally, the affairs of the Holy Mountain are self-regulated by the Great Council, the 'Holy Koinotis', composed of representatives from all the twenty sovereign monasteries, each of which keeps a house in Karyes for its representative and for any of its monks who may be in the town on business. The 'Koinotis' meets three times a week in a simple eighteenth-century house of stone and brick, decoratively patterned, on the outskirts of Karyes where the crooked street runs into the fields. And all the laws and ordinances it issues have the sole purpose of preserving the Holy Mountain from innovations and of upholding the traditions handed down from the past.

There exist, side by side, on Mount Athos, the most varying forms of monasticism. Even the twenty sovereign monasteries follow differing rules. Originally, they were all founded as 'coenobia', which are organised under an abbot, on a communistic basis. In a coenobian monastery the monks are not permitted to own property, and share everything together – even clothes. They have meals in common in the refectory of the monastery, and attendance at services is obligatory.

But with the growth of wealth the demand arose in the fifteenth century for a freer kind of rule, which found its expression in 'idiorhythmy'. In an 'idiorhythmic' monastery there are two classes, the upper performing administrative work and receiving salaries, while the lower class performs the labour of the fields. Government is by a small committee elected by the upper class out of their own number and called epitropes. The monks are allowed to possess property and live in separate apartments taking meals in their own rooms. Even attendance at services is within reasonable limits voluntary.

At the present time eleven monasteries are coenobian and nine idiorhythmic. However, only half the monks of Mount Athos live in monasteries. The rest live either in single cottages, or in organised groups called 'skites', which sometimes look like a monastery, but as a rule consist of many small houses grouped round a central church like a village.

From the very earliest constitutions to the present day, admittance to the Holy Mountain has been expressly forbidden to all women, female animals and beardless youths. The latter provision is by no means observed nowadays. That relating to female animals is still preserved with the sole exception that nowadays hens and female cats are kept by idiorhythmic monasteries. Other animals are still excluded, 'so that their mating may not furnish an outlandish spectacle to souls which detest all forms of indecency, and are daily being purified'.*

*Monk Pavlos of Xiropotamou, quoted by Choukas, *Black Angels of Athos*, p. 204.

The part of the law relating to women has, however, never been slackened. Women have never been permitted on the Holy Mountain. If some have succeeded in living there they have not published the fact. In modern times, various women have tried to enter Mount Athos, mainly from motives of curiosity; but they have had very little success. A year or two ago a Swedish girl came dressed as a man and equipped with her brother's passport. But even on the steamer doubts were raised about her sex; she didn't seem to be quite one thing or the other. And finally, as she was going to land, she had a fit of giggling, completely giving the show away.

Mademoiselle Maryse Choisy, in her seductively entitled book *Un Mois chez les Hommes*, has made far more ambitious claims. She describes the endless trouble she went through in order to enter, the opening words of the book being: 'To start with I had my breasts cut off'. She describes herself being smuggled in, rolled up in a mattress. Once there, she proceeds to have a series of completely improbable adventures. However, to anyone that knows anything at all of Athos, the book is a total and obvious fake. Mademoiselle Choisy was never there.

A Greek girl, 'Miss Europe' of 1930, at least landed on Athos. She came with another girl on her fiancé's yacht, and they both went ashore dressed as sailors at the monastery of Vatopèdi, where I heard the details of this story. The two girls walked about for an hour or two, and one young monk in particular flirted with them a bit, without knowing that they were girls. 'Miss Europe' had herself photographed beside the monk, and when she returned to Athens published the photograph in a newspaper along with the story of her adventure. After some time the newspaper found its way to Vatopèdi. The young monk without saying a word took off his cassock and gave up his whole religious life. He went to Athens in civilian clothes intending to marry the girl. But he found her already married, and his despair at his hopes being shattered was so deep that he went mad. He is still being kept in a sanatorium near Athens.

But who knows if other women have not defeated the thousand-year-old laws of Athos and, unknown to fame, succeeded in living in the one country in the world from which they are excluded?

3
Koutloumoussiou and Iviron

I spent my first night on Mount Athos in the little inn at Karyes. The following afternoon I strolled down to the coenobian monastery of Koutloumoussiou, which lies in a shady valley on the slope of the hill, a mere quarter of an hour's walk from the town. The ground was very fertile round about: not only were there orchards and vineyards, but also many poplars, walnut trees and olives.

According to Athos standards, Koutloumoussiou is a small monastery. At the gateway, the porter took my letter of recommendation to the twenty sovereign monasteries, which I had been given by the Holy Synod in Karyes, and asked if I wanted to remain for the night, and if I were alone. I said I was, which seemed to cause him surprise. However, he told me to go straight into the court, and said I would find a monk to show me up to my room. But there was no one to be seen. And I wandered about without anyone appearing to notice my presence.

It was a curious court, irregular in its shape and arrangement. The church, dedicated to the Transfiguration, stood in the centre. It was painted yellowish red and topped by many little cupolas. The present structure, which is disappointing inside, dates mainly from the sixteenth century, the exo-narthex being eighteenth century. The refectory stood opposite the church (in a corner) and between the two was the *phiale* or sacred well, an invariable feature of Athonic monasteries.

In common with most monasteries on the Holy Mountain, Koutloumoussiou has suffered many disastrous fires, so that the greater part of the buildings round the court date only from the nineteenth century. The very plain but rather picturesque tower, standing in the south-east corner, is an exception, being built in 1508, and the eastern wing of the court is quite a good example of eighteenth-century Byzantine architecture. It consists of three tiers of arcades constructed of bright bricks with here and there bits of inlaid faience.

It was not, however, in this rather attractive-looking wing that I was to spend the night. For, after I had been wandering about the court half an hour, a monk came up to me and offered to lead me to my room which was on the second floor of the south wing – a much gloomier part of the monastery. At first glance the room did not look so bad. It had a nice view over the cupolas of the church, and there were several neat-looking couches round the walls. It was not till late at night that I discovered what horrors the room contained. At this moment I merely deposited the few belongings I had with me (Iorgos was arriving with the rest the following day), and returned to the courtyard.

About 5.30 that afternoon I was startled by the sound of a gong. A monk was hammering on a piece of iron, bent into the shape of a horseshoe, which hung from the roof of the well. Another monk came up to me and asked if I wanted to 'eat bread'. I was hungry, and followed him into the refectory with the rest of the monks. We all sat down at long tables round the walls, while one monk stood in the middle of the hall and read from the Gospels.

The meal consisted of beans swimming in cold, oily water, and some cod-fish accompanied by a tepid oily sauce and celery. In addition each person received a loaf of brown bread, a pewter can full of excellent wine and a handful of raw garlic. The monks ate the latter in enormous quantities with apparent relish.

There were less than twenty monks dining in the refectory, and I wondered where all the others could be. I was not the only guest: a peasant youth and a stout, middle-aged man, very comically dressed, were seated at the next table. The stout man, who turned out to be a wholesale shoemaker, filled his glass with little pieces of bread, which he left to soak. When everyone but he had finished eating, the Abbot gave a sign to the reader to stop. The monks rose, and formed rows near the door, genuflecting deeply as the Abbot walked out past them.

After the meal I wanted to go for a stroll in the orchards surrounding the monastery. But I was called back immediately, as the gates were being closed. In every monastery on Athos the gates are locked at sunset, and must remain shut until sunrise.

I may as well take the opportunity of mentioning here that time on Mount Athos is reckoned not from the hour of midday but from the hour of sunset, according to the old Byzantine system. Twelve o'clock is thus at sunset and varies with the season. Clocks ought to be changed every few days, but this is done very irregularly, with the result that clocks differ all over Mount Athos.

I walked back through the court in the twilight, and found my way to my room. The sky was grey and threatening, the whole atmosphere of the monastery depressing. Nobody addressed a word to me, and I wondered if it was going to be like this everywhere on Athos. Most of the monks had already gone to bed, as they had to get up again at midnight for the night service; so there was really nothing for it but to follow their example. For a while I tried to read by the light of a petroleum lamp, but after a little I decided to make my bed. I had brought my own sheets, blankets, and mosquito net with me from Karyes, and arranged them with the greatest precision on the couch, tucking the net carefully under the sheets to protect me from insects. Then I blew out the lamp and crept into bed.

There was complete silence in the monastery, and I fell into a sound sleep. But after a few hours I awoke with a feeling of itching all over me: things were crawling over my hands and face. I jumped up, searched for the matches in the darkness and lit the lamp. To my horror I saw that my mosquito net was no longer white, but black. The wall behind the couch was covered with black spots, and everything was alive and moving. I set to work to exterminate the invaders. After half an hour the casualty list was 121, but the enemy forces were as strong as ever, and I gave up the hopeless task.

I wandered off through long, dark corridors, feeling my way in the blackness, with a blanket wrapped round me, and finally found a wooden bench on a balcony overlooking some fields. In spite of the discomfort, I managed to doze off; but after a few minutes I was again awakened, this time by a crash of thunder. Great drops of cold rain were splashing on my face, and I had to get up again and resume my pilgrimage through the corridors. A strange hammering in a peculiar rhythm sounded from the courtyard. It was the beating of the *symandron* – a narrow wooden board which calls the monks to the night service. A few dark figures slipped past me, and went down to the church. At last I found a chair in a corner and sat down to get some rest.

Breakfast, consisting of a cup of black Turkish coffee, was shortly after dawn. Lunch, a replica of the dinner the evening before, was in the refectory at 9.30, the usual hour for lunch in coenobian monasteries.

No payment is demanded in any monasteries for hospitality. It is, however, customary to give a small present to the guest master. In some places, even this is refused.

It was without any particular regrets that I left Koutloumoussiou and returned to Karyes where I found Iorgos with the remainder of our luggage. He ought to have arrived the evening before, but the difficulties of the overland journey had been such that he was twenty-four hours late. After my experiences at Koutloumoussiou I was anxious to move on at once to Iviron, to see whether an idio-rhythmic monastery like that would not be more pleasant. So without even waiting to get Iorgos's letter of recommendation we set out to look for mules.

At Karyes, in contrast to the monasteries, it is always very difficult to find mules, unless one is going down at the port of Daphni. We were, however, fortunate enough to meet a youth called Petros, who was taking seven pack-mules to fetch some produce at Iviron. He was a peasant boy from Sikia, a large village on Longos. As we rode, he and Iorgos kept up a long conversation to which I merely listened, while admiring the landscape.

'You had better not go about clean-shaven as long as you are on the Holy Mountain,' said Petros; 'if you do, the monks won't leave you any peace.'

'What do you mean?' asked Iorgos, in an astonished voice. 'Do you mean to say such things really happen here?'

'I should think they do! There's hardly a monk on Athos who isn't like that.'

'Is that why you don't shave?'

'Well, if I did, the monks would be running after me continually.'

'Tell me, Petros, how do you manage to live like this always on the Holy Mountain?'

'Oh, you know, one gets used to the life, and likes it after a while.'

'How old were you when you first came to Athos?'

'Sixteen – now I am nearly twenty.'

'And you were bothered a lot at first?' asked Iorgos.

'I should think I was! They all wanted to go with me.'

'But nowadays, how do you manage to live in a country without women?'

'Oh there are four or five fairly lively young monks, regular clients, who are always at my disposal, and as a matter of fact I have lost all interest in women nowadays.'

'Well, well. That is interesting,' said Iorgos, who in order to ex-tract information was proceeding carefully. 'Tell me more.'

'There is not much to tell; they're all like that, and not easily satisfied either. They want all sorts of refinements. There is one monk in a monastery here who gives me 200 drachmas each time I visit him.'

'Really, in what monastery is that?'

'Ah, I can't tell you. I am sorry, but I promised not to tell. In any case, there is no need for me to give you names and addresses; you'll see for yourself soon enough with which monks there is anything doing.'

I pretended to take no notice of this conversation, but as a matter of fact I had half expected it, because 90 per cent of all modern Greeks are, like the Levantines, bisexual. This fact is not generally known, as the Greeks are tremendous hypocrites. Only people who have lived in Greece, and associated with Greeks of all classes, and speak their language fluently, are able to realise this.

Great friendships between men and boys, such as played so important a part in the life of the Ancient Greeks, are very rare amongst the Greeks of today. Their relations are purely animal. It is supposed to be highly creditable to be the active partner, whereas he who accepts the passive rôle is looked down on. However, in practice the rôles are frequently interchangeable, and there is much lying as to who plays which part.

If one lives in Greece and associates with Greeks one has to accept many things as quite natural which in Western Europe would be considered outrageous. Iorgos had taken me in Athens to see his girl friends, two sisters living with their mother. One of them was studying music at the 'conservatoire', and Iorgos had been on terms of complete intimacy with her. Now he was ready to change over and have affairs with people of his own sex, as any Greek would have been. Knowing this, I made a point of never appearing to adopt a critical attitude or letting him think I was scandalised by his behaviour. My line, so as not to intimidate him, and also to get as much information out of him as possible, was . . . to be merely amused.

Anyhow, Iorgos was not a hypocrite towards me – and I was lucky in having him as a companion on Mount Athos. For, as a mere spectator in the country of males, I could never have gathered as much information as I did about the lives and mentality of the monks. Moreover, many a time finding myself in an embarrassing situation, I was able to escape without offending the monks, by leaving Iorgos to take my place.

To continue: after a little over an hour's ride we arrived at the monastery of Iviron, which lies in an olive-clad valley, a couple of hundred yards from the shore. What impressed us chiefly was its size, with its long, yellowish rectangular walls, topped by blue balconies, that cut into the landscape most effectively.

A hundred and fifty yards before reaching the gates, we got off our mules and did the rest of the way on foot, as is the custom. It is considered presumptuous to ride right up to the gates of any monastery; only important religious dignitaries may do so. We passed through the porch into the courtyard, a huge quadrangle amusingly decorated, and containing a number of trees. There were, as usual, several buildings scattered about the court, but still plenty of open spaces. The main church was yellowish in colour, with here and there Persian plates set into the plaster, and a wide, glazed loggia, the arches of which were filled up with glass, ran along the front. A belfry rose on one side, and high up on its walls was stuck a funny little red and black negro, holding a hammer. Opposite the church was the refectory, also with a belfry, large and modern, containing the library. In a second church is kept a miraculous picture of the Virgin. This picture is supposed to have been painted by St Luke, the Apostle, and the monks relate the adventures it has gone through before arriving at Iviron. It is covered with precious metal and jewels, and an order of nobility, sent by Catherine of Russia, hangs across the breast of the Virgin.

This has been a very valuable picture for Iviron. The Athonic monk Smyrnakes has told us part of its history.* In 1648, when the Czar Alexius Michaelovitch fell ill,

> he requested that the miraculous ikon of Iviron, the Virgin, Portaïtissa, be brought for him to worship. This was impossible; so a copy was made of it. The copy was painted after an assembly had been held by the then 365 fathers of the brotherhood, followed by an all-night vigil. After that some water, in which the remains of saints had been deposited, was blessed. With this water they washed first the original, then the wood on which the copy was to be painted. Then, after reciting a liturgy, the blessed water was given to the priest-monk Iamblichus Romanus, the painter, who worked only on Saturdays and Sundays, while the other fathers held all-night vigils. In this water he dissolved the colours he was to use for the painting of the copy of the Virgin.

*Smyrnakes, p. 480, quoted by Choukas, p. 99.

This copy evidently retained the miraculous qualities of the original, for it cured the Czar, who, in gratitude, made over to Iviron the revenues of the monastery of St Nicholas at Moscow. Until the Russian Revolution this amounted to quite a respectable income.

The ruins of the old tower broke the line of the buildings surrounding the court on the far side, and in the corner to the right was the guest house. We climbed the outer staircase and found the reception room at the end of a long corridor. It was comfortably arranged in a more or less oriental manner with sofas and armchairs, and Russian stoves with high, arched tubes. Portraits of Russian royalty looked down from the walls. We were received very ceremoniously by Father Constantine, the blond-bearded guest master, who brushed aside the difficulty of Iorgos being without a letter of recommendation and declared himself delighted to have us.

Our bedroom was next door. It was quite astonishingly clean. Every day a monk came round and sprayed the beds with insecticide: Iviron seemed to be doing its best to point out to us the contrast between itself and Koutloumoussiou. The contrast was borne out in every way. The table in the guests' private dining-room was laid in the European fashion with a tablecloth, and the dinner provided was excellent, from the hors d'oeuvres, consisting of tomato salad, to the peaches as dessert. The tomatoes were quite marvellous, the finest I have ever eaten anywhere. The wholesale shoemaker of the previous evening had also come on to Iviron, and shared our dinner. He was making a protracted stay on Mount Athos to save money, and remained in each monastery as long as the monks would keep him. He always ate as if he were afraid of being cast out the next day. Father Constantine did not eat with us, but sat at the table making agreeable conversation.

The appearance of luxury was further heightened by an electric bulb hanging from the ceiling. As it was still daylight, the fact that there was no current hardly mattered. Some years ago Iviron was one of the richest monasteries, and a megalomaniac epitrope, who either considered that the dignity of the monastery demanded electricity, or else wished his term of office to be signalised in some striking manner, ordered an electric light installation. Some say that he was cheated, and that the machinery was worthless from the start, others that it was wrecked at the beginning owing to the ignorance of the monks in matters of engineering; at all events the motor did not work, and the monastery cannot afford to have it repaired. Few regret the fact; on the contrary most of the monks regard it as a devilish innovation and main cause of most of the misfortunes which have befallen Iviron of recent years.

The next day we spent lazily, lying on the beach and examining the monastery, and the various manuscripts in the library. In the evening, dinner was rather late. Iorgos and I sat on a bench on the terrace of the guest house, looking over the court. Among the confusion of buildings the red octagonal turret of the belfry with its little negro rose above the pale cupolas of the church. An orange cat was stalking some invisible prey across the leaden roof of the refectory. A few lights were burning on the other side of the great court.

Iorgos kept on humming an air out of *Trovatore*. The blond monk, Father Constantine, came and sat next to him. As they talked it grew dark. Father Constantine began stroking the back of Iorgos's hand; but after a while he rose, saying he had to see how dinner was getting on, and tell the cook to hurry up.

'How boring to have to sit like this in the dark, without being able to do anything,' said Iorgos, and again he began humming the tune from *Trovatore*.

Suddenly he turned to me.

'Did you ever meet a certain Kontos in Athens?' he whispered. 'No? Well, a priest in Athens sent him to Mount Athos to stay with a friend of his in one of the monasteries; I don't remember which now. He gave him 1,000 drachmas for the journey. Kontos spent three months on the Holy Mountain, had a marvellous time, and when he left received a present of 6,000 drachmas from the monk with whom he had been staying.'

Here he suddenly jumped up.

'I can't go on speaking in whispers,' he cried, 'it makes me nervous.'

He walked off, and met Father Constantine in the corridor. They strolled up and down together talking in whispers.

Then Iorgos came back.

'Father Constantine has just been making me all sorts of declarations,' he said, affecting to be unimpressed. 'Not quite what one would expect from a monk! And a year of two ago he actually reported two others, whom he caught *in flagrante*, and they were sent to the island of Amoulianni, off the north-west coast of Athos, which is run as a sort of "concentration camp" for naughty monks. He told me the whole story himself. However, he said he was sorry for what he had done, and that it weighed on his conscience. I should think it ought to – the hypocrite!'

At that moment the attendant called us to dinner, and Iorgos's revelations were broken off.

Besides the shoemaker, Monsieur N., a relative of the Governor, was present that night as a guest. Father Constantine again did not eat with us; he spoke of having to eat with his boys (novices) in his apartment below. The librarian, however, was present to help to entertain the distinguished visitor.

After dinner Monsieur N., the librarian and I retired to the drawing-room. The conversation became very heated on the subject of Ancient Greek pronunciation. It is, of course, a hopeless subject for discussion, as no modern Greek will ever admit that Ancient Greek can have been pronounced differently from Greek as it is spoken today. The final argument was the aesthetic one: that modern Greek (in spite of consisting of a string of i-i-i sounds) is so beautiful that the Ancients could not have spoken their language differently. The party broke up without either side being in any way convinced of the arguments of the other.

As I reached the door of my room, Father Constantine, who must have heard my step, came hurriedly out, muttering a polite, though somewhat embarrassed, 'Good night'. Iorgos was already in bed. Half an hour later Iorgos rose, and crept out of the room on tiptoe towards the apartment downstairs.

After an hour he returned with a bank-note in his hand.

4

Xiropotamou

We had been told at Iviron to be sure not to miss the Feast of the
Holy Cross at Xiropotamou, where representatives from all the
monasteries and skites would be present. To go to this feast meant
completely upsetting our plans, as Xiropotamou lies on the western
slope of the Mountain near the port of Daphni. But we decided that it
would be worth while.

We left Iviron early in the day and went up to Karyes, where Iorgos
had to get his 'letter of recommendation'. Between ten and four the
Synod conducts no business, and so it was already late in the afternoon before we were able to leave Karyes.

There was the usual difficulty in procuring mules, so that we had
to make up our minds to walk, or rather to run, if we wanted to
arrive before the gates were shut. We were taking with us only the
most necessary luggage, some rugs, a mosquito net and the invaluable
picnic case, which had been refilled at Karyes; but even that was so
heavy that, after a quarter of an hour, we sat down under a tree and
ate part of the food, so as to diminish our burden. Fortunately, at
that moment a peasant came along and took our heaviest things; he
was also on his way to the feast and in great spirits.

He trotted beside us, continually urging us to go faster for fear we
should be too late, and talking the whole time like a machine; first
about the wealth of Xiropotamou, which, according to him, is now
the richest monastery on the Holy Mountain after Vatopèdi, and then
telling us at length about having caught recently a *zavkâdi*, a peculiar
kind of chamois, which he had been obliged to let go, as it is forbidden on Athos to shoot these rare animals.

It took us about half an hour to reach the ridge, and from there we
raced down the east slope of the peninsula to Xiropotamou, through
various short cuts among the bushes, in less than an hour. The walk
was magnificent. The hillside fell so abruptly to the sea that usually
one only saw a few yards of land in front of one, with the blue
surface of the sea spread far below the apparent abyss. The sun was

about to set in the crimson sky behind the hills of Longos on the other side of the Gulf.

Suddenly the monastery became visible from above – an immense quadrangle with silvery grey roofs and many chimneys from which pale blue smoke rose gently into the air. A pile of lead-covered cupolas could be seen in the centre of the court.

We arrived to find the gates still open. A monk took us up immediately to a kitchen on the second floor of the western wing, where another monk was stirring soup in a large earthenware pot in an open fireplace. A long, plain table stood in the middle of the room, and on the walls were shelves with plates, pewter pots and wooden spoons. Two small windows in the thick wall looked towards the west. There was still a glow in the sky where the sun had set; the sea was now deep violet.

The monk who had brought us up made us sit down at the table and gave us each some *râki* and a huge glass of water. We were not the only strangers: peasants who had come from far to attend the feast were seated on chairs; on the other side of the table was a very young novice, a boy of about fifteen, who gazed at us sleepily without saying a word. The others asked us the usual questions – what country we came from, how long we had been on the Holy Mountain, what out professions were, etc.

Monks kept passing in and out of the kitchen which seemed to be used as a sort of reception room for minor guests. The house was full. Every monastery on the Holy Mountain, with the exception of Vatopèdi, had sent representatives to Xiropotamou, to take part in the celebration of the Feast of the Holy Cross. And besides these official guests many monks and laymen had come on their own account to be present at the feast. The more distinguished guests, who had announced their arrival in advance, were being entertained in another wing of the monastery.

After about half an hour, when the kitchen was very full, a slender young monk arrived all in a fluster. His name was Chrysostomos, and as his name indicated, he really had a soft, golden voice. He spoke like a flowing brook, gesticulated a great deal, but gracefully, and charmed the whole company by his presence. He took down his long, chestnut-coloured hair, combed it passionately, and did it up again tidily with hairpins. Through having hurried to get in before the gates were closed, he was rather flushed, and kept going over to the window to get fresh air. He had come from the skite of Kafsokalyvia, a painter colony at the southernmost point of the peninsula under the peak of Athos.

All the real guest-rooms had been reserved in advance, and we had to resign ourselves to sleeping in a dormitory with four or five monks. The room was situated at a corner, in the oldest part of the monastery. It was quite picturesque, but it had no beds, only hard couches running round the walls.

It was now eight o'clock (two, by Athos time), and nearly everyone was in church listening to vespers, which always last many hours on the eve of a great feast. In fact, on this occasion, there was to be a practically uninterrupted service all through the night. We were so tired, however, after our long walk from Iviron to Karyes, and from Karyes to Xiropotamou, that all we could do was to sit in the dormitory and wait for dinner.

At ten o'clock (four, by Athos time) we were summoned to the meal. It was a special dinner for guests: the monks of Xiropotamou were going to have their feast-meal the following morning after the service. We were led through long, mysterious corridors, dimly lit by small oil-lamps, to the north wing. Here was the dining-room, long and narrow, brilliantly illuminated by chandeliers set at close intervals on the table, which ran down the whole length of the room in the centre. About half those present were monks, the rest laymen, including a few officials, officers and ecclesiastical guards. One of the epitropes of Xiropotamou sat at the upper end of the table acting as host. Monsieur N., the brother of the Governor, with whom we had had such a violent discussion the night before at Iviron, sat beside him.

It was an extraordinary sight looking down the long row of faces. With only two or three exceptions, everyone present was bearded. Examples of every sort and kind of beard were to be found; probably nowhere else in Europe could such a display have been matched.

Each person had in front of him a pile of seven plates, showing the number of courses there were to be at the banquet. They were as follows:

Cooked chicory salad.
Octopus with onions.
Octopus with chicory.
Snails.
Octopus alone.
Fish roe.
Water melon and grapes.

[35]

The waiters were also monks, and kept running in and out of the hall, with double and treble doses of each dish to satisfy the appetites of many who were trying to take advantage of the opportunity to do themselves well. But the wine jugs demanded most attention, so that they should never be empty.

After dinner most of the guests moved into the official reception room, the walls of which were hung with old-fashioned oleographs of Greek and Russian royalty. But we were very sleepy and the prospect of ceremonial conversation, even though most of those present were somewhat enlivened by wine, was rather dull; so we slipped quietly away to our dormitory.

Although the beds proved too hard and primitive to shelter bugs, we did not have very much peace. Monks were continually moving in and out of the room, coming in turns to snatch an hour of sleep, and then returning to the service. And in the early morning, before sunrise, we were shaken out of our best sleep by a monk who insisted on our getting up immediately and going to the liturgy in the church.

In spite of our sleepiness we rose, and after a secret breakfast of hot chocolate, bread, tinned butter and jam, which we prepared during the few minutes the monk left us alone to get dressed, we went to church.

The service was too dull and the singing too hideous to describe. The sun rose higher and higher, but the monotonous chant of the monks still sounded from the interior of the church, and we wished we had been left to sleep in peace.

5

The Hierarchical College, Pantokrator and Stavronikita

It turned into a hot summer day, and we were thankful to the monks of Xiropotamou for giving us mules to ride back to Karyes. We had lunch there in the inn, and afterwards walked over to visit a school just outside the town – the Hierarchical College.

It is a boarding school founded in 1930, with between sixty and seventy pupils, practically all belonging to some monastery or other. The pupils range in age from fifteen to twenty-five, most of them over eighteen, and are arranged in seven classes. There are eight professors. The courses are like those in a gymnasium, except that more time is devoted to theology. On finishing the course a novice is free to become a monk and continue an ecclesiastical career, or, if he wishes, is eligible to admittance to the University of Athens.

It may at first sight seem strange that it is only since 1930 that a school has existed on Mount Athos. Admittedly before that date certain lectures were given at Karyes, which novices could follow, but they were very elementary and of little importance. In the eighteenth century, however, Athos had a school which enjoyed a certain renown. It was founded in 1749, near Vatopèdi, with the support of the Abbot, and was really an outcome of the educational movement among the laity, which began in the last years of the seventeenth century. The school, which had laymen on the board of directors, did not confine its teaching to theology and ecclesiastical subjects, but included such subjects as logic and Latin in the curriculum. Even laymen were admitted. The school reached its height under Eugenius Bulgares (1753–59), who was specially imported from the school at Iannina. The majority of monks did not approve of the school, particularly of the lay influence. Scandalous charges compelled Bulgares to resign and, in a short time, the school was completely neglected.

This description of Mount Athos from the point of view of

education illustrates the whole attitude of the monks towards learning. In the monasteries (especially those following the coenobian rule) and the cells, it is the ideal that the monks should not only crush the desires of the body by fasting and asceticism, and subjugate their wills by the practice of humility and the most complete obedience, which has an importance even greater than that of prayer, but they must also extirpate the demands of the intelligence. Self-love must be destroyed by unconditional confession and the abolition of intellectual vanity. Knowledge is considered as a barrier to the recognition of divine Truth. The result is that the enormous majority of monks are completely without culture or theological knowledge. They can scarcely read or write, and are only acquainted with the rule of their monastery and the lives of a few saints.

The view from the college over olive fields sloping gently towards the sea had a rare charm. There was a wooden pavilion with a few cypresses near by, from which one could see a monastery far down below; it was Iviron, where we had had such a warm reception and had been asked to come back soon.

But we decided that afternoon to ride down to Pantokrator – one of the smaller monasteries on the east coast, a few miles north of Iviron. The track was very rough. We rode for about an hour through brushwood and shrubs of thyme. Then, all of a sudden, we caught sight of the monastery – a picturesque pile of buildings lying below us on rocks, washed by the sea. Two small red* Byzantine cupolas rose in the middle of the disorderly and irregular expanse of roofs, dominated by a massive medieval tower.

Pantokrator has a little harbour at the south, in which rowing boats and small sailing boats are kept. We first rode down to this harbour, and then climbed up again about fifty feet to the entrance of the monastery.

In front was a paved terrace, shaded by a huge mulberry tree, with, on the right, a wooden pavilion. Every monastery on Athos has a similar pavilion in which monks sit and chat during their leisure hours.

The view from the terrace was magnificent, looking right along the

*On this point I have doubts: cupolas on Mount Athos are normally of lead, and the word 'red' may be due to a typist's error. At all events it sounds more picturesque, and anyhow by now the cupolas of Pantokrator have become quite rosy in my memory. I hope this note will be taken as a proof of the painstaking accuracy of every passage in this book!

coast to the south. About two miles distant the walls and machico-lated tower of the monastery of Stavronikita rose on a rock high above the sea, and beyond, soaring up to the sky, was the superb marble pyramid of Athos. Few mountains in Europe can be com-pared to it for beauty, and nowhere does it appear grander than from Pantokrator.

In practically all Greek monasteries the church is in the centre of the court, thus destroying its effect; but at Pantokrator the church is at the far end of the oblong court. Several orange trees grow out of the pavement.

The guest-rooms placed at our disposal – a bedroom and a private dining-room – were at the south-east corner of the monastery on the top floor overlooking the sea. The view from their windows was the finest to be had from Pantokrator, or for that matter anywhere on the Holy Mountain.

A very old monk brought us our meals to our rooms. In spite of his long beard, he looked like an old woman. Although he was fifty-eight, and looked more like seventy-eight, he told us he was one of the youngest of the monastery. He had been there only twenty-eight years. We asked him if he were pleased to spend his whole life in one place without ever moving.

'What can one do about it?' was his only answer. 'A monk is like a soldier, without liberty or choice. He must obey and do what he is told.'

Next morning we decided to walk over to Stavronikita, which was only two miles off, and spend the day there, returning to Pantokrator in the evening. We were told that the real road ran inland, rising to a height of four or five hundred feet before descending again to the monastery. But the weather was so fine, and the water so tempting, that we made up our minds to follow the coast. We could see a fisherman's hut about half-way along, and were sure it would be possible to make our way over the rocks if the path stopped. There was, however, no path, and soon we were wading over slippery rocks with the water up to our waists, carrying our clothes and photo-graphic materials on our shoulders. When finally we could go on no further even like that, we tried to climb up through the tangled brush-wood and steep rocks to the path. But after half an hour we had to give up the attempt and return to our starting-point. Then we set off again on the proper track.

The walk is among the most charming to be taken on the Mountain. Here and there we passed little hermitages, where monks, many of them Rumanians, lived in twos or threes. Each house had its terrace garden, with melons and grapes hanging from pergolas; 500 feet below their walls the blue sea washed the base of the hill. Springs of fresh water came trickling out of the Mountain slope under shady ilexes, and the bright fruit of orange and lemon trees gave colour to the varied vegetation.

On crossing the little pass, the landscape became less precipitous again. In the foreground were fields of silvery olives and behind was a low ridge covered with bushy green pines. The marble Mountain rose in the background. And down to the left, like a medieval castle perched on the rock, 200 feet above the sea, stood Stavronikita.

In its present form it dates from 1540, although existing before. As a group of buildings it is extremely picturesque and one of the few monasteries on Athos which have any claim to architecture. Passing though one of the arches of the half-ruined aqueduct, which connects it with the hillside, we approached the entrance. There was no sound but the trickling of water; not a soul to be seen but the sleepy porter in his lodge.

Here, as at Pantokrator, the original courtyard was extended on one side in the eighteenth century, so that the church is at one end. But in spite of the extension, the court is extremely small, and its area is further reduced by the tower, a very fine crenellated structure built about 1546. This tower stands in the court independent of other buildings.

The parlour of the guest apartment was a comfortable room in Turkish style with divans running round the walls. We found we were not the only guests. There was also an Orthodox priest from Jerusalem, who, besides Greek, spoke fluent Italian, Arabic and a little French. He was aged about thirty-five, with a well-trimmed beard and a complete set of gold teeth. He spoke in a high, affected voice, and when he smiled, hid half his face bashfully behind his hand.

'It is amazing how these monks live here on Athos,' he began at once, speaking Italian so that the old monk in whose apartment he was living and who was present should not understand. 'They are saints. They have renounced completely the outer world, and are satisfied and happy to live here in peace and prayer. But I am different, you know. A month of this life is as long as I could stand; after that my head would start going round. I am used to my freedom. Here the monks have to obey the laws of the monastery, and only get leave to go away about once in eight years. In Jerusalem we get leave when we want. Last summer, for instance, I went for a few weeks to Cairo to see my parents, then I went back to Jerusalem, and after a month set off again on an escapade to Athens and came over here to the Holy Mountain . . .' The father giggled behind his hand.

'Just imagine. These monks never wash: they disapprove of it. I could not live without baths. Why, if one doesn't wash one's body it begins to smell after a while. But the other day when I asked this old monk here for some hot water to wash with, he was quite horrified and couldn't understand why I should want to do such a thing.'

Father Arsenios puffed out his chest, full of consciousness of his superiority.

Iorgos was bored by this conversation which he could not understand, and was sitting on the sofa glancing through the visitors' books full of poems and sentimental remarks written by all sorts of travellers who had stayed in the monastery. Father Arsenios joined Iorgos on the sofa, and kept on slipping his hand under the visitors' book which Iorgos was holding; but the young man, who was in a bad temper, jumped up and went to look at the view.

'Why is he so cross?' asked Father Arsenios, and I pretended the reason was that there were no cigarettes to be had in this monastery.

'If', said the father, 'your friend is so upset at not getting exactly what he wants, he won't find life on Athos a bed of roses.'

6

Vatopèdi

The great idiorhythmic monastery of Vatopèdi is the richest on the Holy Mountain. It is celebrated for its luxury and its modern innovations. This is the only establishment on Athos where time is reckoned in the manner of the rest of the world, and where the old calendar has been scrapped. It has electric light and Western sanitation. Monks from other monasteries invariably speak scornfully of Vatopèdi, and refuse to send representatives to its feasts as a protest against its 'advanced' ideas; but there is often a tinge of jealousy behind their words and one of them described it as the 'Paris of Athos'.

The road from the south passes through hilly country, covered with trees, mostly chestnuts, planes and ilexes, until at the edge of a steep ridge one sees a wide amphitheatre lying before one round the edges of a long bay, the only one on Athos. Wooded hills surround it, and the lower plain is full of charm with rich and varied vegetation, a picture of rural prosperity. The monastery itself remains hidden from view, owing to a fold in the ground, until one is almost underneath the walls.

Before we got so far, however, we had a foretaste of the grandeur of Vatopèdi. A clatter of horses' hoofs was heard, and a sound of laughter. A cavalcade of six or seven horses appeared round the corner, led by a fairly young man in black silk robes, with carefully tended hair and immaculate hands, negligently holding the reins of his trotting mule. He kept turning round in the saddle, smiling and making apparently witty remarks to a companion, a pace behind. Mules with servants and baggage followed. The young man was leaving for a holiday. Nothing could have been more like a rich, completely worldly, medieval prelate, on his way to pay a visit. The mules vanished from sight in a cloud of dust. Only a trace of perfume lingered in the air.

Our arrival at the monastery was hardly observed. There was everywhere tremendous activity and bustle. Silk-clad monks, servants and peasants kept moving in and out through the long dark entrance passage, past the series of gates. The gateway itself was covered with flags, coloured ribbon and garlands of laurel branches, and the path leading down to the shore was decorated with arches of leaves. Inside the court were further decorations and flags.

The courtyard is immense, a huge irregular triangle, neatly paved, sloping up the hill with a peak at the top and dominated by a massive tower. It is so large that in spite of the confusion of buildings in it, the refectory, the storehouses, the wells, towers and churches, there still remain wide, open spaces, with here and there a few trees. And all around are buildings in the most fantastic variety of architecture, of every period and style, with here classical pediments and there open arcades three of four stories high. They are almost all painted in bright colours, red or blue, or striped red and white, and make an effect of extraordinary gaiety.

When we were sitting on the beach after lunch, we saw a long procession of monks in gorgeous robes coming down from the monastery to the sea, where a large boat with many pairs of oars was being prepared. It was evident that something out of the ordinary was happening, and in any case the elaborate decoration of the monastery could hardly be a daily event, even at Vatopèdi. We inquired. A visit was expected that afternoon of the Crown Prince of Sweden in a yacht. And indeed we could make out a yacht far out at sea. The dignitaries of the monastery got into the boat and were rowed out to meet the Prince. The yacht approached, but appeared to have difficulty in making up its mind what to do. The rowing-boat stopped about half a mile from land, everyone on board standing. But the yacht suddenly turned and fled at full speed in the opposite direction, and there was nothing for it but for the elders of the monastery to return, reform their procession and go back again by the decorated pathway without their guest.

The feast-meal of six courses (four being mutton prepared in different ways) was none the less successful, and the Prince's name was entered in the visitors' book as a kind of spiritual consolation.

The following morning we looked at the church of Vatopèdi, which is one of the largest on Athos. From the outside it is a very confused-looking mass, painted dark red. The exo-narthex is a two-storied building, with an open arcade on the ground floor (an unusual feature) and is attached at the south end to the bell-tower, which is obviously no part of the original plan. Very little light penetrates into the interior of the church, every inch of which is covered with dark frescoes painted in 1312, the best example of the so-called Macedonian School on Athos. The large dome is supported on four black granite columns brought from Constantinople. They are, however, almost hidden by the numerous chandeliers and sacred pictures encrusted with shining metal. The great iconostasis is resplendent with gold, but the carving in this dark extravagant interior is too rich and heavy.

While we were sitting in the arcade of the church, a young monk called Lucian, whom we had met the evening before, came up and asked us if we were going to the wine feast.

'Come along, boys! It is the last day of the vintage, you know, everyone is in the fields. There'll be lots of fun – dancing and singing.'

We followed Lucian out of the monastery. The sun was still fairly low and the sky a deep blue. We climbed the hilly country behind the monastery, at first though fields and olive-groves, and then through woods of evergreen oaks. Every now and then we came across other monks, also on their way to the feast. After about half an hour we reached an immense vineyard, where many peasants and monks were picking grapes. They seemed very jolly and much freer than any other monks I had seen on Athos. Everybody was busy picking, loading or eating grapes. Most of the monks wore large straw hats; others had transformed their usual black caps into the appearance of helmets, by attaching a peak in front.

We crossed the field, picking our way among the vines, to a peasant-house which stood in the centre of a little grove of cypresses. Fresh water came rushing from a fountain between two fig-trees, and beside them was an open fireplace, where the feast-meal was being cooked in a cauldron three feet wide. String beans and lumps of mutton were stewing in a sauce of celery, parsley, tomatoes and onions. The cook, an old monk with a long, grey beard, kept stirring the food, and every now and then threw in a terrific handful of pepper. No one seemed to have any idea when the meal would begin.

Behind the house the thickly wooded hillside rose steeply, but in front the ground dropped down in terraces to the sea. The landscape was quite un-Greek in character. No wild mountains with glowing faces of bare rock; only a broad cultivated valley with wooded slopes, olive plantations, vines, fig-trees, walnuts, cypresses, and parasol pines. Judging by the silver olives, the cypresses and the pines, one might have been in Tuscany, for the Greek olive-tree is usually darker and larger than the Tuscan, and the Greek pine shorter, bushier and brighter than the typical Italian parasol pine.

After some time a train of mules appeared, some laden with pewter plates and jars, some with loaves of bread. The peasants and monks began to collect round the cauldron, but we were invited to have lunch with the epitropes and more venerable monks in the peasant-house, upstairs, on a sort of roofed terrace. The meal was almost a repetition of the banquet of the night before – rice, soup, boiled mutton, stewed mutton with string beans, roast mutton with laurel leaves, grilled mutton cutlets, cheese and grapes. The wine was sweet and very strong.

The white-bearded epitrope beside me kept handing his empty glass over his shoulder to the serving monk, crying: 'Wine, more wine!' On the other side of the table, Iorgos sat next to a police officer, who kept rubbing his leg under the table and whispering that he had something important to tell him afterwards. The noise from the crowd down below grew louder and louder as the wine went to their heads. Every now and then a deaf and dumb man gave blood-chilling yells of pleasure. Suddenly I heard the sound of a clarinet, the first musical instrument I had come across on Mount Athos. Running downstairs, we found all the peasants grouped together waiting for the chief epitrope to give permission for the dancing to begin. A moment later he looked over the edge of the balcony and gave them a sign. As a special concession dancing – a thing normally forbidden – was allowed at this semi-pagan festival.

The clarinet player began piping wild intoxicating themes. The group of peasants all took each other's hands, holding handkerchiefs, and began dancing in a row. The man at the left was the leader, and kept performing the most extravagant twists and turns and jumps, while the others followed with a uniform rhythmical step. Every few minutes a jug of wine was handed to them. The monks sat round gazing at the dancers: even on this day they were not allowed to join in. Their eyes twinkled, and a few movements and occasional steps showed that they would have loved to take part in the dance – a very common form of amusement in Greece. The elders watched from the balcony above; suddenly one shouted: 'Here, 100 drachmas for wine!' and threw down a note. The crowd shouted; the pewter mugs were refilled a number of times. The piper played more wildly than ever. The dancers became tipsy and their movements more and more erratic: one or two had to stop and simply rolled on the ground. For two hours the dance went on.

[45]

Long before it ended, Iorgos and Lucian had disappeared together across the fields and were lying side by side among the vines. The older monks noticed the incident and whispered comments to each other. Lucian was just nineteen, and had only been a year at Vatopèdi. He once came on a visit and, liking the life so much, decided to become a monk. He said he adored girls, and really became a monk because girls like monks. He seemed to think he would have far greater success now than if he were a layman. He dreamt of having a virgin, he said; but he could hardly expect to find one at Vatopèdi after all!

After some time the two returned, and we walked back, Iorgos singing songs and Lucian holding his hand all the way.

The day was so hot that Iorgos and I decided to go and bathe. As we passed the gateway of the monastery we saw the police officer in the belvedere waiting for Iorgos. We pretended not to notice him and went down to the sea, following the coast to the south past some fishermen's houses, until we came to a bay hidden from the monastery.

We undressed and lay in the sun, but after a short while the police officer appeared along with a companion. We tried to ignore them, and swam out; but they swam round us, and when we came out of the water they insisted on starting a conversation. I ran off down the beach, leaving Iorgos to their mercy.

The police officer made all sorts of advances, openly calling attention to his amorous agitation, and at last crying:

'Look, Iorgos! It is you that are the cause of this. Wait, Iorgos . . . please . . . come here! . . . Just a minute! Do you want money? I will give you as much as you want.'

But Iorgos ran off and joined me. We dressed quickly, and Iorgos explained to the policeman that we had to take some photographs before the sun got too low.

'Very well,' whispered the officer, 'then I shall be waiting for you at nine, this evening, beside the gateway of the monastery.'

Iorgos did not answer, and we walked back to Vatopèdi.

In the courtyard after dinner we met Lucian, who asked us to come with him to Father Sophronios's rooms, where, he said, he spent most of his spare time.

Father Sophronios was a strikingly good-looking man of about twenty-eight, though his large, dark beard made him seem older. He had come here from Gallipoli, a boy of sixteen, as companion to an uncle who was a monk, a common practice on Athos.

The rooms of Father Sophronios's exceptionally charming apartment overlooked the court. They were like the rooms in an Oxford or Cambridge college. The study was simply but well furnished, and had a large balcony. The bedroom next door contained a spare bed for visitors. On the other side of the passage was the kitchen, overlooking the fields.

Father Sophronios provided the customary coffee, *râki* and sweet jam.

Lucian sat on a couch beside Iorgos, and very shortly began stroking his face.

'Don't touch my face,' said Iorgos.

'Why not?'

'I can't bear it.'

Lucian went on, however, becoming more and more tender. Father Sophronios, who sat beside me, pretended to be a little shocked. Then Lucian put his hand inside Iorgos's open shirt front.

'Aren't you ashamed of doing such things in front of strangers?' asked Iorgos.

'Not in the least, because I love you.'

Lucian caught hold of Iorgos's head and whispered something in his ear.

'That is the one thing I never do,' answered Iorgos in a loud voice.

Lucian went on whispering, and suddenly began to pull Iorgos's hair about. They started wrestling together; then they went into the bedroom.

After about a quarter of an hour they returned, both looking rather embarrassed. No one knew what to talk about. We decided to return to our rooms in the guest-house. It was ten o'clock.

Hurrying down the staircase and across the dark court, Iorgos whispered to me: 'Do you realise that the chief policeman has been waiting for me for over an hour at the entrance gate?'

We let him wait.

The following morning we went to the 'liturgy' at 6 a.m. It was an ordinary weekday and, as is often the case, one of the chapels in the court was being used for the service. Lucian was in church in a black silk robe, with a long train and a large black veil over his cylindrical cap. He kept swishing about from one end of the transept to the other, rustling his black skirts and muttering prayers. His manner was so solemn and engrossed that it was hard to believe it was the Lucian of the day before. But for an instant when the other

[47]

monks were not looking, he glanced at us with a smile, and winked. Then immediately his expression became as severe and immovable as before.

7
Interlude at Chilandari

We spent the following night in the monastery of Esphigmenou, about two and a half hours north-west of Vatopèdi. It is a picturesque-looking square block, washed by the waves of the sea, and shut in on the land side by three wooded hills. Its situation is its most interesting feature.

The guest-master and his assistant went to every trouble to entertain us, but when we attempted to give the customary gratuity on leaving, the guest-master refused to accept it, adding with slight huffiness: 'We are a *coenobian* monastery,' thus expressing his sense of superiority to the monks of Vatopèdi.

After a walk of less than an hour from Esphigmenou we came to the Serbian monastery of Chilandari, lying like a great fortress in the quiet valley surrounded by hills thickly wooded with fat ilexes, bright green pines and dark cypresses. The forest round about is completely unspoilt and probably the finest to be found on Athos. Delicate wooden balconies ran round the monastery above the ancient walls of yellowish stone and pink brick. In front of the gateway was a charming open square with a few trees, walnuts, oleanders and one enormous cypress.

A Serbian monk met us in the porch and took our letters of introduction We passed through a series of gates connected by a dark, gloomy passage as in a medieval castle, and suddenly turning a corner found ourselves in the courtyard, bathed in bright sunlight. It was a most effective entrance. The court was magnificent, and neither gave one the impression of being crushed in between high walls, as in the smaller monasteries, nor of confusion or carelessness as in so many of the larger. It was warm and friendly; one breathed freely. The wide paved space sloped gradually down towards the far end, where the church stood, its long side facing the entrance. Four huge cypresses grew beside the decorative marble *phiale*. The church had admirable proportions, and was decorated with fine designs in tile work accentuating the lines of the architecture. On the east side of the court, among charming buildings of stone and brick, rose a magnificent twelfth-century tower.

While our luggage was drawn up by a pulley to the second floor of the guest house, we were shown up the half-open staircase to the reception hall where we were offered jam and *râki*. The walls were covered with photographs of the Serbian royal family and of innumerable Serbian heroes and patriots. All the monks spoke Serbian with each other, and for a moment we felt in another country. Afterwards we were shown to our bedroom. It was very clean and comfortable. A private dining-room adjoined. Our windows looked down over luxurious kitchen gardens: silver-green cabbages, French beans, celery, cucumbers, marrows and glowing scarlet tomatoes lit up by the morning sun shone fresh and tempting against the brown earth. Opposite, the dark wooded hills rose steeply, but through a gap to the north one caught a glimpse of the sea and the far-off mountains of Thrace.

The country round Chilandari is full of charming walks. After lunch I went down to the sea to bathe. For about a mile I followed a wide path of soft earth which curved gently alongside the course of a stream. Planes and huge walnut trees grew irregularly on each side, forming a kind of avenue. It was noon, but a gentle wind came from the direction of the sea. Insects hummed, and birds sang and flew from tree to tree. The ground was covered with cyclamens and autumn crocuses. After some time the path came to a high tower, where a medieval Serbian princess, whose son had become a monk at Chilandari, had been allowed to live. She had been unable to bear the separation from her son, and so the ground on which the tower was built was declared secular. She never left it, but each day could wave her hand to her son on the battlements of the monastery.

The path there left the stream and cut across open pasture land towards the sea. Rolling hills covered with pines and holly-oaks rose of each side. It was an ideal pastoral landscape. One was filled with a delicious feeling of freedom. Not a soul was to be seen. Wild pigs with long legs, high arched backs and big ears, ran across the path. Oxen and he-goats grazed under the twisted old olives, and horses rolled in the grass.

On reaching the sea the charm remained unbroken. The water stretched like a glittering mirror to the mountains of Thrace, glowing pale blue in the slight haze. On a promontory to the left stood the walls and towers of the ruined monastery of St Basil; in front a small rocky islet rose from the sea, scarcely a ripple disturbing its verge; to the south the long soft hill of Thasos spread along the water. A flock of cranes flew overhead and settled on some rocks near at hand. Orange sails glided past over the deep blue sea.

For several days I remained at Chilandari, enjoying the country round about and the peace of the monastery itself. Life there moved uneventfully on in an extraordinary calm.

The monastery, originally built for 1,000 monks, is still fairly prosperous, but it is sad that it should be so empty. It contains only fifty-three monks, some of them Russian and Bulgarian, and even of that number nearly half are so old and frail that they are permanently in the hospital.

On my last evening I made an exploration through the kitchen gardens. In one part I found a large pool full of tortoises swimming about and enjoying themselves. About a dozen had crawled out, and were having a sunbath on the other side, looking like miniature prehistoric animals. Their shells were extremely flat and green, their necks unusually long. They kept opening their mouths and yawning in the sun. Beyond the end of the cabbage forest some buffaloes, of a kind I had never seen before, were drinking from a little river. Nearly all the animals in this part showed curious characteristics, and I was sorry not to see any of the wild boars and jackals which live in the neighbourhood.

On the other side of the river the ground rose very steeply. I scrambled for half an hour through holly-oaks, pines and thorny brushwood to the top of the ridge. The sun had sunk low behind me. In front, beyond a series of rolling pine-clad hills, was the sea. The mountains of Thrace were now pink with soft-blue shadows. A salt wind brought great clouds over from the distant horizon. The cypresses waved. It was lonely; silent, except for the sound of the trees, and the birds' singing. But over there, on the other side of the water, was the world of people, of events. The sun had almost gone; I slowly returned to the monastery with its aged monks.

8

Four Northern Monasteries:
Zographou, Kastamonitou, Dochiariou
and Xenophontos

The ride from Chilandari to the Bulgarian monastery of Zographou, across the central ridge of the peninsula, is the finest which can be made on the Holy Mountain. At first we climbed for an hour from the valley through a pine forest with soft brown pine needles underfoot. The blue sea sparkled behind us through the trees.

From the summit the view was magnificent, looking north to Thrace, with endless rows of hills rising behind each other; and to the south one could see right along the ridge of Athos to the white peak rising far in the distance. Then the path, which from this point was paved, descended again towards the east, passing through a forest of evergreen oaks.

We had been riding down the valley for over an hour when we suddenly caught sight of an immense block of white buildings rising among the trees on the opposite slope. This was Zographou, the monastery of the Bulgarians.

Approaching it from below one is impressed by the height and solidity of its stone walls. Yet it has something extremely cold and pretentious about it. Zographou is, indeed, the ugliest monastery on Athos. It was completely rebuilt, regardless of cost, towards the close of the last century, not in the pleasant traditional style of most modern restorations on Mount Athos, but in a proud self-conscious nineteenth-century spirit. Nevertheless it is greatly envied by the monks of other monasteries, who regard it as the architectural showpiece of the Mountain. On entering the courtyard we found two magnificent cypresses, but they hardly mitigated the depressing atmosphere of the monastery.

We were again in a foreign country, but this time not in a friendly one. The Bulgarians were offish, and had none of the touching kindness and open-heartedness which was always so striking in other monasteries. The food we were given that night was practically uneatable, especially after the delicious fare of Chilandari. The guest-room we were allotted was unclean, but even so we preferred to sleep on the hard floor rather than on the beds.

Next morning we left in a hurry, and rode on south over hilly country to the monastery of Kastamonitou, which is nearer to the sea, though not within sight of it.

Kastamonitou as it now stands dates also from the nineteenth century, but it forms the most striking contrast to Zographou, being small, unpretentious, almost attractive, like a large farmhouse. In no way, however, is the monastery of interest.

We were received in a sort of Turkish room, with a divan running round three sides, and old-fashioned, coloured prints on the walls of Greek warships, Byzantine Emperors, and King Constantine of Greece going for his morning ride with his sons. It was the nature of Kastamonitou to be old-fashioned.

But we were back in friendly Greece. The guest-master, a rather pathetic old man, set out to be agreeable, but, alas, the food he brought us was even worse than what we had had at Zographou. We were given a soup consisting of sticky flour and water covered by a layer of nauseating oil, followed only by potatoes fried in some horrible stuff of mysterious origin. The guest-master sat opposite us to watch us eat with an expression of fatherly benevolence on his face. He so evidently thought that he was giving us a treat that Iorgos and I had to make every effort to eat the food. It was, however, too much to ask of us, and while we distracted the monk's attention elsewhere we threw some of it away and stuffed our pockets with bread to eat afterwards in private.

We decided it was better we should leave at once. The monks seemed quite upset. One old man, with a snowy beard, came up to Iorgos, as we were saying goodbye at the entrance, and kissed him on the neck behind the ear, saying: 'Won't you stay with us just *one* night?' But our minds were made up, and we set off for the next monastery.

We rode down to the sea and then followed the coast until after a hour and a half we reached the monastery of Dochiariou, lying charmingly near the water against the steep slope of the hills. Olives, cypresses and some orange trees grew round about.

We found Dochiariou architecturally to be one of the finest

monasteries on Athos – second only to Chilandari. The court was long and narrow, rising in terraces on the land side to the graceful tower which enclosed it at the top.

No one at the monastery paid any attention to us. When we first arrived everyone was asleep, but when the monks awoke physically they remained mentally in a state of somnolence. We realised that their neglect of us was not unfriendliness, merely sleepiness and indifference.

It rained a good deal while we were at Dochiariou, but we were partially consoled by the charm of the guest apartment, above the terraced part of the court. It was decorated in a delightful eighteenth-century Turkish style. From the windows we looked over the roof of the high, buttressed church to the sea beyond. Our room was the cosiest we found anywhere on Athos, and Iorgos was so enamoured of it that during the whole three days we remained at Dochiariou he hardly ever went out. He performed all the time a continual toilet, washed clothes, and also did a bit of secret cooking, as, alas, the food was even worse than at Kastamonitou. Our guest-master, who had a long cotton-wool beard, bits of which we always felt tempted to pull off, fed us exclusively on a kind of large yellow pea, normally given only to chickens.

The main event of our stay at Dochiariou was a thunderstorm one evening after dusk. In the passage leading to our room we came across two young novices who were standing in front of a window holding a candle and talking to each other in whispers. They obviously did not belong to the monastery. We soon found out that they were on a pilgrimage round the Holy Mountain, and had just come to Dochiariou for one night. It turned out that one of them had been a sailor, and that Iorgos had known him while doing his service in the navy. They at once started an animated conversation about common friends, punctuated from time to time by terrific crashes of thunder. Every few seconds great flashes of lightning lit up the curious turrets and cupolas of the church, behind which white waves could be seen on the black sea.

The young novice seemed very moved by the storm, and told us that as a sailor he had on three occasions been in storms at sea so tremendous that each time he had made a vow to become a monk if God spared his life. Twice he had failed to carry out his vow, but after the third storm, in which his ship was nearly wrecked, he came to Mount Athos with the definite decision to give up the world and adopt a monastic life. He had already been several months on the Holy Mountain, and spoke with enthusiasm about the life. He had not yet made up his mind in which monastery he would settle down, and was visiting them all in turn, to see which suited him best.

I was struck by his religious fervour. This type of novice is rare on Athos, as most young monks are brought to the Holy Mountain as boys, by an uncle or some other older monk, before they have ever had the chance of knowing the outer world, or of discovering whether they have a real vocation for a monastic life or not.

When the thunder finally ceased the old monk with the cotton-wool beard appeared with another candle and called away the novices, showing them to a room at the far end of the corridor. We went to our room and opened the windows. The rain had ceased. It was very dark. There was no moon; only one star was visible between the clouds above the crenellated tower. There was a scent of orange blossom in the air. Somewhere in the fields below a cat was whining . . .

I blew out the candle and got into bed.

Before leaving Dochiariou I asked the porter if he could tell me the legend about the foundation of the monastery – I had heard about it. He turned on me indignantly. 'A legend!' he shouted. 'What do you mean? It is absolutely true!' And he told me the story in almost exactly the same words as it is given in Rycaut's book, published in 1679.

A poor Boy, attending the little Flocks of this Monastery in the Fields, accidentally found a Stone with an Inscription thereon, directing to a place of hidden Treasure; after the reading of which, the Prior sent some Kaloires with the Boy to discover it and bring it to the Monastery; which having found, they designed it for themselves and appropriated it to their own peculiar benefit, without other account thereof unto their Prior: to which end they threw the Boy from a Rock into the Sea, with a Stone about his neck, who falling called upon S. Michael: which having done, and secured the Treasure, they returned home, and reported that the Boy had feigned a false Story, and for fear of punishment was run away. The next morning early the Clerk of the Chappel entering into the Vestry to light the Lamps, found the Boy cold and wet, and half dead with the stone about his neck, of which acquainting the Prior, he came in haste, and learned the whole truth of the Story; for which cause he punished the Kaloires, recovered the Treasure, and therewith enlarged the Monastery, and again consecrated it and dedicated it to Saint Michael, by whose favour and protection the poor Boy was conserved.

A small coastal motor-boat took us in half an hour to the large coenobian monastery of Xenophontos. It is a conglomerate mass of buildings round an irregularly shaped court, in which there are two churches. The smaller dates from the sixteenth century, as does the refectory. The larger was built about a hundred years ago by an innovating abbot, who succeeded in providing his monastery with the largest church on the Holy Mountain. Other building schemes of his were never completed, and the inland sides of the court remain surrounded only by bare walls with chimneys and windows built into the upper stories, showing where new ranges of cells were to have been constructed.

9

St Pantaleïmon: The Russians on Athos

A monk rowed us in an hour and a half in a small boat to the Russian monastery. The coast was all the way dull and very steep, without vegetation except for a few olives high above. Finally, on rounding a small promontory, we beheld what seemed a large village lying by the sea. It was like a dream. The boat glided on the water; in front was a confusion of great white buildings mounting irregularly, with magnificent trees growing among them. The bright red roofs were topped by turrets and green cupolas. We seemed to be arriving at some fantastic barbaric town, rather than at a monastery. But on approaching closer, some of the splendour faded: many of the buildings became more like enormous warehouses at the docks of London or Hamburg. We climbed from our boat on to the broad deserted quay. Our short journey seemed to have transported us hundreds of miles to some foreign country. Here everything was different from what we had come to expect of a monastery on Athos. It was nearly mid-day. Not a soul was to be seen. Our boatman from Xenophontos helped us to carry our luggage up a broad paved way, shaded by immense plane trees, till we came to the porter's lodge. The gateway he looked after could hardly be called the gateway of the monastery, as here at St Pantaleïmon the buildings were all scattered and unconnected as in a village. It gave access only to the principal part, containing two churches and the refectory. The porter was a very old Russian who hardly spoke Greek. He directed us to a long building opposite the gateway, on the other side of a large esplanade. So we carted our luggage across to the big barrack-like building cut off from the court by a dry moat covered by a series of iron bridges. We entered the building on the second or the third floor, we could not be sure which, as the ground sank on the side facing to the sea.

We found ourselves in a wide passage, but stopped short, horrified by the sight of three diseased and deformed creatures advancing towards us. One had a completely hairless, furrowed skull, and a withered, paralysed leg, which made a scraping sound as it was dragged across the floor. He had the expression of a murderer become insane through twenty years' solitary confinement. The second had no nose and a permanent ferocious grin. The third was still young. He was unnaturally thin. His pale, yellow skin was stretched so tightly across his sharp bones that it almost seemed as if it might split. Even his beard was pointed. He held his head crooked with the look of a frightened animal. There was something incredibly tragic, and at the same time gruesome, in his expression. Iorgos wilted at the advance of the three chimeras, who mumbled Russian together. He whispered, 'If this is the guest house, I am leaving the monastery on the spot.' We caught sight of a staircase, and fled to the floor below. It was a mysterious building. We never managed to find our way about properly as each floor was exactly the same in plan, and wherever one happened to be there always seemed unlimited possibilities of rising higher or of descending. On the top, as a matter of fact, there was a church .

Now we met another rather less terrifying monk. We plucked up courage to ask him where the guest-master was and he pointed to a door. For a long time I knocked. At last the door was opened by a short, gnome-like creature of extraordinary breadth, presumably the guest-master. He took our letters of introduction, fetched some keys, and showed us to a rather bright, clean-looking room, with two beds, a table, some chairs and a still-life hanging on the wall. We were agreeably surprised.

'Well,' he said, looking at us suspiciously, 'what do you want now?'

I murmured hesitatingly that we should be very grateful if we could have something to eat.

'Hum!' he grunted and walked off.

Iorgos and I looked at each other.

'Perhaps visitors aren't given any food in this monastery,' said Iorgos. We waited.

After about half an hour the guest-master returned, carrying a large tray covered with small dishes. I nearly gasped at the sight of such an elaborate meal. There was bortsch, boiled rice, sardines, freshly fried potatoes, sour cucumbers, bread and tea. Tea! They were all practically new dishes for us since we had been living on the Holy Mountain. Our spirits revived.

After lunch Father Vassilis, a monk of about thirty-five, with a red beard and spectacles, came to see us. He spoke fluent German.

His father, I discovered later, had been a Cabinet Minister in Russia before the war. Father Vassilis told us that a great feast was to be celebrated in the monastery two days hence.

We decided, therefore, to go up to Karyes that afternoon, to change our baggage and get more films, and to return to the monastery for the feast. We were given two mules and were accompanied by Father George. There are of course several Father Georges at St Pantaleïmon, as at every monastery. Ours was known as the 'mechanician'. On our way, which led at first through a fine forest of oak overgrown with ivy, Father George told us about himself. He was a Baltic Russian, and naturally spoke German. After finishing his studies as an engineer, he worked for a couple of years at the Opel works in Berlin, but later returned to Russia and settled at Sebastopol in the Crimea, where he married. He developed consumption, and was told by the doctor that he had only a few weeks to live. It was then that he was converted and became a fervent Orthodox. He had expected to die, but lived. His cure came about of its own accord, and he regarded it as a miracle and decided to become a monk. But the war broke out; he had to become an officer in the army and was employed as a military engineer. On the outbreak of the Revolution, however, he fled and came to Mount Athos. Since then he had never written to his wife, nor to any member of his family. There was no one who knew where he was.

The path was now rising steeply, winding through small brushwood and rocks. On one side we passed a large modern Russian church, surrounded by a few houses. I felt a little embarrassed at letting this elderly monk of fifty-five or sixty, who had once been an officer and an engineer, walk while I rode on a mule. But as a matter of fact it was less comfortable and more trouble to ride than to go on foot. We had to keep beating and kicking the animals to make them move at all. Later I found out that they were the oldest mules the monastery possessed. No wonder we had the feeling that they were liable to break down any moment. The surprise was that they were able to carry us at all. Just before reaching the top of the ridge, the path entered a second forest, this time of chestnuts, and skirted a charming little mountain lake, looking extraordinarily fresh among the trees. A solitary Russian monk stood at the edge fishing.

This whole part of the Mountain, as far as Karyes, belongs to St Pantaleïmon.

Until the Great War, Russia used Mount Athos as a spearhead

for its nationalistic designs in the Aegean. It endeavoured to play a leading part in Athonic affairs by buying up cells dependent on other monasteries, and subsequently enlarging them on one pretext or another until they surpassed their parent houses in size and number of inmates. The Czars expended immense sums of money on lavish building schemes and vast endowments, so that by 1900 there were about 3,500 Russian monks on the Holy Mountain, that is half the total number. Since the Russian Revolution, however, the monks are completely cut off from their previous source of supplies, and are compelled to live on the income derived from the wood they own on the mountain itself. Although their numbers have sunk to 650, they are now the poorest monks on Athos.

On Saturday afternoon we rode back to St Pantaleïmon. This time we had better mules, but it was again Father George, the 'mechanician', who accompanied us. All the way he spoke about religion. He was a very earnest Orthodox, and believed that the whole world would shortly be converted to the Orthodox religion. He inquired particularly about the progress of the Greek rite in Germany, as, according to a precious manuscript written by some saint and kept in the monastery of Pholotheou, it was predicted that Germany would be the first country to be converted. The time was believed to be at hand.

We reached the monastery an hour before sunset and found it this time quite lively. Groups of monks, mostly old men, were to be seen everywhere. New arrivals were pouring in to assist at the feast, mostly from the various Russian skites, a few from other monasteries. There was a continual movement on the esplanade.

We went to our room and dined, but were shortly roused by the sound of bells, the first we had heard on Athos, as many monasteries do not have any and the others only ring them on rare occasions. I ran out on to the esplanade. Crowds of monks were flocking from all sides to the gateway of the inner precinct. The sun was setting. It was 12 o'clock (Athos time). The great service, the 'Agripnia', was about to begin.

As I approached the central building, the sound of the bells became more and more terrific. I joined the throng passing the archway and crossed the inner court. The service was to be held in the largest church of the monastery, on the top of the north wing. Three long flights of steps led up to it. The sun had now set behind Longos. A new moon glittered in the deep green sky. The sea was striped with bands of purple and carmine. Looking up, I could see in the twilight the biggest bell in the belfry slowly moving up and down. It seemed that I had never seen a bell so immense. The sound was overwhelming, like a tempest, and the tone of the bell so deep, so unearthly, so different from anything I have ever heard that I felt myself transported to another world. Other bells clashed higher and wilder, while others sounded shrill and intoxicated against the background of thunder.

It was no longer Greece. The power of the Empire of all the Russias seemed to be expressed in this torrent of barbaric sound. Here the fallen Empire still lived. My feelings had never been stirred in such a way, except perhaps by the Coronation scene in *Boris Godounov*.

Suddenly the storm stopped. The stillness was almost sinister. Only the deep unearthly sound of the great bell went on reverberating for several minutes in the black silence. Night had come. Hundreds of monks, like phantoms in the darkness, kept climbing the stairs. I mounted with them.

The church was very large. It had a regular nave and had no division into narthex and church proper as everywhere else on Athos. Hundreds of candles and oil lamps were burning round the iconostasis, and the metal parts of the numerous icons glittered in their light. I seated myself in a choir stool. The service was just beginning. The prayers were answered by a hidden choir, singing in four voices. The basses sounded extraordinarily deep, the tenors amazingly high. The music was full of strange modulations. I was very tired and returned to the guest house to sleep a little after following the service for about an hour. Shortly before midnight Father George came and woke me, and led me through the pitch darkness back to the church. The bells were again thundering and clashing, calling the monks to the second part of the service. The moon had set, there was no light except from the stars. In the darkness the sound of the bells was almost frightening.

The choir was now visible. It consisted of about twenty monks, one of whom conducted and acted as leader. A series of old Russian songs for four voices were sung. They were very beautiful and very sad. I have rarely heard such sad music. It was, however, extremely impressive to hear such fine singing, as in all the other monasteries on Athos singing in unison is enforced, and even that is usually very carelessly performed. It is a mere monotonous sound, tending often to be a cacophony.

[61]

Nearly a dozen priests, wearing gorgeous robes, each different from the other, officiated at the religious ceremony in the candlelight. It lasted three hours, and when it was finished all the monks came one by one in an endless procession and kissed a specially sacred icon. The Abbot gave them his benediction.

Father George now came and took me along with him across the court and esplanade to the chapel on the top floor of the guest house, where another service was to be held in which he took a certain part. By the time this was finished it was nearly four o'clock, and I went back to my room to sleep. But at six I was again awakened by Father George in order that I should hear the liturgy in the main church. By eight it was over and the monks collected in the court, waiting for the feast-meal, which soon followed in the refectory. The hall was modern, in the traditional shape of a cross. Every seat at every table was occupied, the Abbot being seated on a platform at the end of the nave. There was bortsch, followed by codfish swimming in lukewarm oily sauce, bread and plenty of wine. As a dessert came a curious dish of small balls of flour containing lumps of pink sugar and raisins, which is eaten in Orthodox countries after funerals and sometimes on religious feast-days. A choir sang all the time. When the meal was over, the monks – most of them old men with grizzled beards – returned to the court and began saying goodbye to each other. Many had old, faded clothes. There was something infinitely pathetic in the whole scene. A large number had come from distant skites which they never left except for occasional feasts. As they departed some were given loaves of bread at the gateway to take with them. Others sat for a long time in the sun, on benches outside, talking, almost motionless, making few gestures. Finally, one by one, they too departed. By noon the last had gone. The heat and the silence were oppressive. Of the events of the night, no trace remained. The monastery had died out.

Gregoriou: The Brigand Speaks

The monastery of Gregoriou is built on a mass of rock, washed on two sides by the sea. Immediately behind it rise the hills of the west coast.

The hot midday sun was beating on us when we arrived in our little rowing-boat at the Arsenal and carried our luggage up the steep paved way to the monastery. It was the hour of rest, and no one was to be seen except the porter in his lodge, who directed us to the guest department in the inner court.

After taking a light meal of food we had brought with us and having a swim, we were received by the guest-master, whose period of rest was over. He was a cheerful monk called Theodoros, who had gone to America at the age of seventeen, returning after a couple of years to become a monk on Athos, where he had been for the last thirty years. He brought us the usual coffee and liqueurs. We had run out of money, and I was wondering all the time whether a money-order had arrived for me at Karyes or not. Iorgos, who like most Greeks did a good deal of fortune-reading in one way or another, offered to read my coffee-cup. I was just turning it upside down when Father Theodoros appeared and said:

'What are you looking at? You are reading your fortune in the dregs! You shouldn't do such a thing: it is an old woman's habit. Here in the monastery it is strictly forbidden. If we are caught reading our fortunes we are severely punished.'

'Don't you believe in it?' said Iorgos. 'Don't things come true which you see in the coffee dregs?'

'Of course they do,' said Father Theodoros, 'but it all comes from the devil: that is why it is forbidden in monasteries. It comes from the devil.'

He quickly took our cups away to the kitchen.

Afterwards we went down to have a look round the court, which was narrow and irregularly shaped, and full of charm. The church and the refectory, connected by a rough cloister, nearly filled the side facing the sea. At the corner, however, beside the church, there was a back door to the monastery, leading on to a little platform above the sea, with a cemetery and a tiny frescoed chapel, the only building spared by the fire of 1761. Opposite the church was a large block of striped brick and stone, in part arcaded, with a well-proportioned eighteenth-century belfry tower. But what gave the court its special character and attractiveness was the side against the mountain. Here the ground rises suddenly and is covered with the ruins of the original monastery buildings, which were burnt down. Even of the great tower only fragments remain. Nothing has been rebuilt. The old foundations rise in a series of terraces connected by open staircases. One of these has been converted into a diminutive kitchen garden, while the others are roofed over by vine pergolas. A little stream comes rushing down from the mountain; it has been canalised and turned into a fountain.

Among the ruins and vines we found a little hut where a monk with a dark face and big bushy black beard was working mending shoes. He was at one and the same time the shoemaker, the blacksmith, the chemist and the nurse of the monastery. He took quite a fancy to us for some reason, told us his name was Savvas, and insisted on our visiting his cell. It was on the top floor just beside the bell-tower, with one window looking over the roofs of the monastery to the sea. The only furniture was a narrow hard couch, a chair, a tiny table, and a wooden chest, like seamen have, and on the walls were charcoal and pencil drawings of sailing ships, and an icon of the Virgin. Father Savvas made us sit down and pressed caramels, plum jam, coffee and liqueurs on us. Then he produced a dozen small apples. They were very good and no sooner were they finished than a second dozen appeared. Father Savvas was extremely jolly, always laughing, and terribly happy with his life at Gregoriou. He asked lots of questions and told us the story of his life, munching apples as he spoke.

'I was born in a village of Maina, about thirty miles south of Sparta,' he said. 'While I was still quite a small child, my parents died and I was looked after by an aunt. When I was twelve, I got a job on a caique, carrying goods from one part of Greece to another. The sea always had a fascination for me. My father had been a sailor, all my family in fact. And I expected to pass my life on the sea too. Even now, as you see, I sketch ships in my spare time.' He nodded to the drawings on the wall, and polished another apple between his hands before starting on it.

'My career as a sailor', he went on, 'did not last long. When I was thirteen we were sailing past Mount Olympus. The wind was poor, and we had no provisions on board. So we anchored by the coast, got out and went off in search of food.

'In my eagerness I rushed on ahead. There was no path; just rocks and shrubs, and here and there pine trees. It was getting dark, and I thought my companions were close behind. I called out to the others, but no one answered. I shouted again and again, as loud as I could. But the only answer I got was the echo of my own voice from the rocks above. I didn't know what to do. Should I go back to the coast, or go on to the village? But where was the village? I had no idea where I was. Everything looked wild and sinister in the twilight.

'I was terrified at finding myself alone in this wilderness. The silence was uncanny; then suddenly I heard wolves howling in the distance. I set off running in the opposite direction, but tripped over the rocks and lay on the ground sobbing. Then, exhausted by the long climb, I fell asleep.

'Day was breaking when I awoke. I was terribly hungry and decided that the best thing was to make my way back to the boat. But after a few minutes' walking, I saw a man with a black beard, dressed in the *fustanella*, standing in front of me. He had two pistols and a belt full of bullets.

'"So you've been sent to spy on us," he said with a fierce look. I couldn't understand at first what he meant. He ordered me to follow and led the way to a cave nearby.

'Then I realised that I had fallen into the hands of brigands. The famous bandit Kolias, the chieftain, was squatting with six others on a carpet in one corner of the cave. I told them my story, but they wouldn't believe me and insisted that I had been sent as a spy. After a council of war they came and told me: "If you try to run away we will kill you; but if you join our group, you will have lots of money and everything you want."

'So I remained. My companions, as I found out later, searched for me for three days and then sailed away, thinking I had been devoured by wolves.

'Olympus, you know, is the highest mountain in Greece – it is really a whole complex of mountains. Well, we lived up there in caves. We had beautiful rugs, and soft cushions to sleep on. When we woke up in the morning, we saw the sun rising out of the sea and the whole world seemed to lie beneath us. The air was fresh and bracing.

There was always game to shoot, and any amount of money. We really had a splendid life.'

Before coming to live on Olympus, he went on, Kolias had spent several years with his group of brigands in Euboea, on the slopes of Mount Delphi. Once they went down to a village and sat in the inn, drinking and playing cards. Nobody knew, of course, that they were brigands. The son of a rich German who owned an estate in the neighbourhood came in while they were there. Kolias started drinking with him and soon they all became very jolly. Kolias invited the youth to come and have another drink with him at his house. He said he had horses ready, and it was only a few minutes' distance. The youth accepted, but no sooner had he mounted one of the horses, the brigands pointed the pistols at him and told him to ride on without uttering a word:

'If you shout, we will shoot you dead,' they said.

They brought the young man to the mountain, and sent a message to the father to say that he would get his son back untouched if he sent them three mugs full of gold coins. If he refused, they said he would only receive his son's head. The money was sent, and the boy returned, but during his short stay with the brigands he got to like the life so much that he was quite heartbroken to have to leave.

Father Savvas, noticing that we had finished the apples, opened his trunk and took out another two handfuls which he gave us to eat.

I asked him how long he spent on Mount Olympus with Kolias.

'Eleven years, my boy. And I never got tired of the life up there. You see that photograph on the wall there? That was our group.' He pointed to a small photograph glued to a board in the corner of the cell, showing a number of smartly dressed men in a sort of uniform more suggestive of soldiers than brigands.

'Once when I had been at a village getting some provisions, I came across a Greek youth who was a photographer, and brought him back with me. He stayed a week at our camp and photographed us all.

'It was shortly afterwards that we were attacked by soldiers. They came from all sides, and killed many of our men. Those that were left, including Kolias and me, had to surrender. We were sent to prison on Aegina. I was very shortly set free. But Kolias and the others were kept for months and months.

'One day I went over from Athens to the island of Aegina to visit Kolias in prison, and brought him some fish as a present. He had been living on bread and water, and he was so touched that he told me of a certain place on Mount Olympus where he had hidden a lot of money.

'I went there at once and found it, and for the next years lived with it in Athens. I bought a motor-bus and ran it between Omonia Square and Galaxidi.'

'And what happened to Kolias in the end?' I asked.

'They were kept in prison in Aegina for many months, then they tried to escape. One day when the guard entered their cell, they jumped on him, took his keys, and left him bound and gagged on the floor. Then they ran into the prison yard. But they were seen by a policeman, who fired at them. Kolias was wounded in the chest. He managed to run on for another fifty yards before dropping, and when he lay on the ground he ate the grass in his wild rage at being beaten. Then he died.'

'And how did you come here?' I asked.

'Well, I lived for nearly two years in Athens. But I couldn't get accustomed to the life. I was unhappy. I had no peace within me. My parents were dead. My brother and sister did not even know me. Finally I went to a priest and confessed my evil deeds to him. The priest told me I would never find peace anywhere unless I became a monk. So I came to Mount Athos; that was seven years ago.

'Only the Abbot knows the dark secrets of my life ... Ah, it is a great satisfaction to confess. The moment you have confessed to a priest, you are no more troubled by your conscience. You feel so released and happy.

'My boy, you should become a monk,' went on Father Savvas, turning to me. 'Once you are a monk on Mount Athos, you have no more worries of any sort. Why, look, if you lead a life in the world, you are sure to marry, and then just think of all the troubles and worries you are bound to have, the need to earn enough to support your wife and nourish your children, and buy them clothes, and send them to school, and pay doctor's bills – there is no end to it. Here there is nothing like that. Your soul is absolutely free and happy. The Virgin Mary looks after you and protects you.'

He took up the conversation again in our room on the morning of our departure.

'One has no more desires, my boy,' said Father Savvas. 'One gets used to everything: one's body calms down in course of time. When I go up to my cell in the evenings I don't have voluptuous thoughts any more; I take a book, instead, and read about the saints. . . .

'You know, when someone enters the garden of the Virgin Mary, he acquires a positive disgust for women. Ships sometimes stop quite near here and I see women in the distance; and once or twice the Abbot has sent me on board the steamer at Daphni to fetch something or other and I have seen women then. But each time I get more and more disgusted at the sight. Since I came here, neither a woman nor a boy can give me feelings of any sort.'

'A boy, did you say?' said Iorgos. 'When you were with the brigands up on Olympus, did you do anything of that sort?'

'No, no. Such things are forbidden up there. There was a belief that if you did them your luck would turn against you, and you would get shot. In the villages below the mountain there were peasants. We used to go and take the most beautiful girls, and violate them.'

We were nearly ready to leave; our packing was finished. Iorgos had taken off his shirt and was about to put on another.

'And here,' he said, turning round, 'have you never done anything at all?'

Father Savvas had a sudden burst of excitement: his arms shook.

'We want to,' he cried, 'but how are we to find anyone?'

A few moments passed in silence.

Then Father Savvas sunk forward, his head between his hands:

'Oh . . . I have sinned, I have sinned.'

Simópetra, Dionysiou, St Paul's

We came from Gregoriou to Simópetra by sea, landing at the Arsenal. The monastery rose high above like a white fairy-tale castle, perched on a precipitous rock in the centre of a wild gorge; and the nearer one came to it the stranger it appeared, with the upper half of its long façade barred by rows and rows of flimsy wooden balconies.

The entrance is at the back, which is joined to the mountain-side by an aqueduct consisting of three tiers of arches, and is much lower than the front. The proportions of this part are admirable: the walls bold and irregular, the windows small and placed far apart.

The entrance passage, dark and vaulted, is paved with rough stone; it slopes steeply upwards and turns a corner before reaching the courtyard which is actually on the sixth floor of the monastery. Staircases lead down to the apartments on the lower floors.

The courtyard is different from most. Although it is very small, it is not, as is only too often the case, in any way gloomy or shut in, partly owing to the fact that the surrounding buildings are only two stories high, instead of three or four, and partly because there is a small gap on the south-east side through which one has an extraordinary glimpse right down to the sea. The church is a harmless dark red building connected with the south wing of the monastery.

Simópetra has lived through great disasters, the last being the devastating fire of 1891, which left practically nothing standing. The monastery was rebuilt on the old foundations between 1892 and 1902, in part with the help of a donation of £14,000 from the Czar of Russia. It is surprising with what good taste the new buildings have been designed. Certain parts are really excellent and, apart from a few minor details, there is nothing ugly about it.

We were given very spacious rooms in the guest-apartment leading on to a balcony, the highest of many which run round three sides of the monastery. We found ourselves on the seventh floor – the eleventh if the lower part of the monastery had windows. From our balcony it seemed as if the wall fell directly into the sea 800 feet below. Simópetra is hardly a place for people who are apt to be giddy, as one cannot avoid constantly walking along these rickety wooden balconies which take the place of corridors and provide the only means of moving from one room to another.

The view, however, is staggering, although limited to ninety degrees by the precipitous walls of the mountains. Cliffs of rock rise above each other on each side, and one has a sensation of being suspended in the air between these oppressive walls. To the south, the view extends from the conical summit of Athos on the left to the southern point of the sister peninsula of Longos on the right, while the houses of the Nea Skite and St Anne's can be seen clinging to the steep slopes of the Mountain.

In a way the most impressive and sensational part of Simópetra are the privies. They are extremely primitive. A section of one of the balconies on the north side has been enclosed with wooden walls, as a screen, and a huge hole has been cut in the floor, as if it were designed for giants. Looking through it, one sees a vast rocky abyss, which makes one reel, so that one is in serious danger of falling through. To make use of the privy is an acrobatic feat, because a notice in large letters on the door warns one on no account to make a bad shot.

We had to pay a flying visit to Karyes – to the bank and to buy provisions – before going on to Dionysiou. We spent one night in the little inn and then returned the next day by the same path. It was a long walk of over four hours, following the ridge of the peninsula for the greater part of the way. The day was rather stormy, and at times a wet mist came down and blotted out everything from sight. The vegetation was semi-alpine – mainly a forest of chestnuts and firs. All one heard was the wind, and occasionally the creaking of trees. Water dripped from the leaves, and the ground was sodden underfoot. Once we passed a solitary old monk, tottering along slowly towards Dionysiou, but after that for over an hour we saw no sign of a human being.

Then we met two workmen and a young monk, going in the direction of Karyes. The two workmen greeted us in the usual way, but the monk kept his head bent towards the ground. Suddenly, however, he came running back and shouted to Iorgos:

'Hullo, old girl, what brings you to the Holy Mountain?'

'Who are you? I don't know who you are,' said Iorgos.

'You old whore!' said the strange little creature, wriggling his hips.

'Don't you remember me two years ago in Athens, when I used to sell little painted icons?'

Iorgos then recognised him. Turning to me, he told me the little monk used to sell things at the door of a variety theatre in Athens, where he had been dancing at one time.

He asked him what on earth he was doing as a monk, and the creature replied: 'Oh, I just decided to become a nun, you know. Haven't you got a cigarette for the poor girl?'

The 'poor girl', who couldn't have been much more than seventeen, said he was now living at the skite of St Anne's with the prior, but that he really wanted to settle in one of the great idiorhythmic monasteries. He was just then on his way to see what place would be best for him. His monastic name was Josapha.

Josapha had an extraordinarily depraved face. All his movements were extremely effeminate, and he showed continually his delight in wearing a skirt. He spoke in an affected falsetto voice, making all sorts of extraordinary squeaks and gurgles. Suddenly, pulling up his skirts, he began to dance in a rather indecent manner.

We couldn't help laughing at the grotesque creature, who seemed like an apparition from some other world in this solemn damp forest, high up on the ridge of the Mountain, with here and there patches of white mist lying among the trees.

The two workmen with whom he was going to Karyes now called him from the distance, so he collected his skirts and ran off, uttering a prolonged 'O-o-o-oh . . .' in a falsetto voice. Then he turned round once more and shouted, 'Praise God,' and vanished from sight among the trees.

We walked on through the chestnut woods, treading the damp, yellow leaves. The silence of the Mountain descended on us once again.

We spent that night at Simópetra and walked back the following morning to Gregoriou, where we found a motor-boat which took us to Dionysiou. In summer, when the weather is fine, most of the traffic along the west coast is by sea.

The monastery of Dionysiou is built at the mouth of the gorge of the 'Aeropotamos' (Windy River), down which there is nearly always a wind blowing. It is an unfriendly spot, without vegetation. Here are no oranges, no cypresses, no fig or olive trees – only one solitary vine growing opposite the gateway.

Like Simópetra, Dionysiou stands on a small point of rock; but

[71]

while at Simópetra space has been gained by building upwards and producing a kind of skyscraper, at Dionysiou all extensions have been made outwards. Whole ranges of apartments project out into the air, supported only by frail wooden buttresses. They are very precarious and top-heavy-looking, but at the same time picturesque.

The court is very crowded and the church painted scarlet red. But inside, the church is one of the more effective of those on Athos, partly owing to the drum of the cupola being lower than usual. It is crammed with lanterns, pictures of madonnas and saints, even hung with flags. The doors, inlaid with ivory, leading from the exo-nathex to the narthex, and from the narthex to the church proper, are very remarkable. And Dionysiou has perhaps more frescoes than any other monastery. Not only is the whole church painted in rather fine sixteenth-century work, but the T-shaped refectory is entirely frescoed.

The monastery was founded in 1380. A certain Dionysios, a native of Kastoria and for some years a hermit on Mount Athos, saw a miraculous light burning on the site of the present monastery. He took this as a sign from Heaven and presented himself at Trebizond, where his brother, who had previously been a monk on Athos for twenty years, was Metropolitan. He succeeded in gaining the sympathy of the Emperor Alexios III, and the latter agreed to provide funds for a monastery on the spot where Dionysios had seen the fire, and where he had already built a tower. Alexios gave 100 loads of silver for the work, and in return the monks had the duty of praying for all the members, past, present and future, of the Imperial family, and of providing hospitality to all natives of Trebizond who should visit the monastery for scientific or devotional purposes.

The Golden Bull of Alexios (c. 1380) with the portraits of the Emperor and Empress Theodora is still preserved at Dionysiou; but of recent years it has been shown to no one except the Archbishop of Trebizond himself. An elaborate facsimile with a golden seal is shown to visitors instead.

Comparatively little is known about the empire of Trebizond. Alexios I, the lineal heir of the Comneni, made this city the capital of a kingdom on the Black Sea with the help of a number of noble fugitives from Constantinople, after the latter's capture by the Latin Crusaders in 1204. Trebizond retained its independence until 1461, when it surrendered to the Turks.

The coastal motor-boat, run by monks, took us on to the last monastery on the west coast – St Paul's. From the sea it appeared quite impressive, situated a bit inland, under very wild cliffs – but as we walked up to it over the stones of a wild desolate ravine our expectations were disappointed.

St Paul's is almost entirely modern, built in the barrack style. Inside everyone was asleep. We were starving, but it was impossible to get anything to eat. For a long time we had to wander through long, bare whitewashed corridors like in a hospital, until finally a monk appeared and showed us into one of the guest-rooms, telling us to lie down on the beds and sleep, as it was the hour of rest. But when we lifted the covers on the beds we found the sheets crawling with animals. It would have required more asceticism than we could muster to spend the night there, so after looking at the tall, simple, seventeenth-century tower and a small frescoed chapel, which were the only things spared by the great fire of last century, we decided to push on immediately.

12

The Land of the Hermits

The next monastery after St Paul's is Lavra, right on the other side of the Mountain, on the east. The normal way to go is by motor-boat, and during the summer, when the weather is fine and the sea calm, there is a fairly regular service. It is, however, far more interesting to take the land route: the wild mountainous track passes through some of the finest landscape on Athos, the part least known to travellers. It is the country of the hermits.

The path leads through several skites and hermit settlements, such as St Anne's and Kerassiá, where it is possible to spend the night. As the path between St Paul's and St Anne's is too rough even for mules, the Abbot of St Paul's gave us two young peasants to row us from the Arsenal, where we had left our luggage, to the harbour of St Anne's.

The sea was as calm as a lake, and on rounding the first promontory we passed below a group of about thirty houses with chapels built into them, standing in the bright-looking gardens. An abandoned tower rose among them. This was the Nea Skite, founded in 1760, an idiorhythmic dependency of St Paul's, containing about 100 monks. It looked like a scattered village, half-buried in luxuriant vegetation. To the south great orange rocks tumbled into the sea, as in parts of Capri.

We now rowed into the harbour of St Anne's. A monk with a couple of mules was unloading some sacks. He took our luggage on ahead while we walked. The land rose in a steep amphitheatre covered almost to the water's edge with fine trees, much more southern in character than the vegetation elsewhere on the Mountain. The olives were larger and there were light green pines as in southern Greece. After climbing these fertile slopes for over half an hour, we came to the first houses of the skite, small primitive white buildings of one or two stories with slate roofs and an occasional wooden balcony. Nearly every house had a curious little flat dome at one end, over the chapel.

St Anne's, a dependency of Lavra, is the oldest of the idiorhythmic skites. Its legendary history goes back to the year 1000, but in its present form it was founded in 1680. There are about 50 houses and about 150 monks.

Here, as in all other idiorhythmic skites, the monks live in separate houses, in twos or threes, occasionally in larger groups. They enjoy even more freedom than in an idiorhythmic monastery. A Prior, the *Dikaios*, is elected annually to preside over the skite and represents its interests in all official matters. He lives in a special house beside the principal church, the *Kyriakon*, where services are held on Sundays and feast days. The Prior is expected to provide hospitality to visitors to the skite.

St Anne's seemed a 'garden-city'. The houses rose in terraces above each other, each one standing in the centre of a plot of flowers and vegetables, and embedded in masses of orange and lemon trees, figs, peaches, olives, cypresses and oleanders. Here and there among the vegetables and trees heavy with fruit grew a few immense dark ilexes. And behind the houses rose a wall of grey and orange rocks like the cliffs of Delphi. Near the church a basket full of bones lay against some upright stones under a peach tree. On top were two crossed thigh bones with a skull placed carefully against them. At first sight it seemed as if someone had just laid the basket down for a moment. But instead it was really tied to the stone, and on the skull was a message written in red paint reminding the passer-by of the transitoriness of human life.

By the time we reached the Prior's house, the sun had set. A pretty terrace connected the house with the main church and offered a magnificent view of the whole amphitheatre with the sea, now crimson, 1,800 feet below, and the dark outline of the hills of Longos beyond.

The Prior's house was simple, but the vegetable soup we were given for dinner in the large kitchen was better than many we had tasted. We slept outside on a kind of veranda, but neither the cold nor the hard couches were sufficient to frighten the bugs we had hoped to avoid by not sleeping in the usual guest-chamber.

Next morning, before starting off, we looked at the church, a charming early eighteenth-century Byzantine brick and stone building with a belfry beside it; the walls of the church had recesses with pointed arches showing Islamic influence. The interior was curious, the transept being longer than the nave, but the proportions were very nice, above the average on Mount Athos. The church contained a celebrated miraculous icon of the Virgin, black with age. The legend is that on placing a coin against it, it will stick if the person is good, but if the person is wicked, the coin will fall to the ground. The miracle worked. But I did not learn whether I was good or wicked, as my coins sometimes stuck and sometimes fell – perhaps because I am neither one nor the other. The miracle can hardly be due to magnetism, because among those that stuck were coins of aluminium, copper and nickel. After a few minutes, however, they usually fell down again.

We arranged for our luggage to be sent directly to Kerassiá, about two hours distant, while we ourselves made a detour in order to pass by the hermit settlements on Karoulia and Katounakia. Before leaving St Anne's we called at the little house of Father Kallinikos, the only monk with cigarettes for sale, on the outskirts of the settlement. We found him on a terrace in front of his house hanging up washing under a pergola of cucumbers. Father Kallinikos looked like a portrait of a Chinese mandarin. He was very friendly and did everything to make us stay, but our luggage had already gone, and we had a long day's walk in front of us; so, after a short chat, we had to say goodbye. Before we left, however, he insisted on giving us a large loaf of bread and some walnuts, which, as it happened, saved us that day from starvation.

The track followed the curve of the amphitheatre, rising gently as it approached the southern edge. Crocuses grew underfoot among the grass and stones. Sometimes the way was a mere ledge in the rock, sometimes it broadened out, passing through bushes with here and there big evergreen oaks. It is one of the grandest walks on the Mountain. After three-quarters of an hour, we reached the corner, the last point on the west coast of Athos. A little to the right of the path was a platform of rock with one house and a chapel, called Little St Anne's. We wandered round the house to a terrace at the front, 1,200 feet directly above the sea, with an extraordinary view right along the west coast, showing Simópetra and even the steep slopes further north. As we sat there eating nuts a fair young monk appeared and offered us coffee, *râki*, and caramels. He was called Father Onophrios. He sat down and began to tell us about the life at Little St Anne's and certain other isolated cells. It is very hard and the main diet of the monks is dry bread and a little tea. But they usually live to a great age, 100, 120 or even 125 years. Father Onophrios was extremely kind and warm with us; he asked all sorts of questions about events in the world and apologised for not being able to put us up, as there was nothing to offer us to eat. He advised us to go on to Father Daniel, who had a far more comfortable house; but before letting us go, he insisted on presenting each of us with a round wooden carving in intaglio, made by himself, for stamping designs on bread. He refused to accept a penny for them, although they were his only source of making a living.

The country was completely barren after turning the point, with only a few bushes and stunted wind-blown trees. The day had begun to cloud over. Ahead were a few widely scattered white houses, the settlement of Katounakia, where Father Daniel had his house – a fairly large building with a wooden balcony running along the front and a chapel adjoining. When we arrived, Father Daniel came out on to the balcony to greet us, with a palette and paint brushes in his hand. He remembered at once having seen us at the feast at Xiropotamou, and invited us into the studio, filled with easels, pots of paint, brushes and books. Five other monks, also painters, lived in the house, On the walls were conventional pictures of saints and innumerable studies of hands, which the monks seem to paint as if they were still-lives. We were invited to stay, but we wished to see Karoulia, a hermit settlement down by the sea, part-Greek and part-Russian. It was too steep for there to be a real path, and we had to scramble over rough rocks. Half-way down we met a frail little creature dressed in rags looking like a gnome. He was bending down cutting herbs with a large knife. He said his name was Seraphim, and asked us to visit his house. He was so jolly and lively that we promised to come and see him after looking at the Russian settlement. We found it very uninteresting, however, as it consisted only of a few tin-roofed houses. It was only later that we learned that a former university professor and a relative of the late Czar were living there, whom we were sorry not to have seen.

We returned at once to Father Seraphim who was still gathering his herbs. He led us across the steep rocks towards what seemed to be nothing but a cliff. But after going along a narrow ledge, and up some steps cut in the rock, past a tiny chapel, no bigger than a cupboard, we saw a white wall ahead, forming part of the precipice below. The rock was cut away behind and formed a covered passage a few feet wide. Three cells opened off the passage. Beyond the cells the passage came into the open again, forming a terrace with an extraordinary view. It was completely solitary; only the grey sea and the heavy, clouded sky were to be seen. Looking over the edge of the terrace one saw 100 feet below a mass of wild rocks near the water, over-grown with cactuses. A solitary peach tree clung to a ledge. Behind Seraphim's terrace was a cave with festoons of onions hanging from the roof; the further side was shut off by the kitchen.

Here we were introduced to a young hermit, Father Gabriel, who shared the house with Father Seraphim. A sick kitten lay at his feet. While we nursed it, Father Seraphim told us how he had come to Athos from Thebes forty years ago; and how he had first lived in this extraordinary dwelling with an older monk, who had been dead thirty years now, who had built it on the cliff-face and decorated the little chapel in the rocks.

Father Gabriel was an extraordinary contrast to the strange wizened hermit, young and strong. During the course of the conversation I asked him how he had chosen to become a monk. He said he had come from Dimitsana in Arcadia and had been a policeman in Athens for a few years. One day he had caught a Communist and brought him to the police station where he and the other policeman beat him and maltreated him horribly. The Communist was condemned to many years' imprisonment. He was of good family, and his mother, a distin-guished Athenian lady, used to visit him in prison. Gabriel became interested in their refined prisoner, and began to wonder if he could have deserved the punishment he had received. So one day he went to visit him, dressed in civilian clothes. He was not recognised by the Communist and they had a long talk together. Gabriel came away convinced of the goodness of the prisoner's character. A few weeks later the Communist died in prison, mainly as the result of the beating he had received at the police station. Gabriel was terribly distressed at being the cause of his death, knowing he could have let him off free, had he wished, when he had caught him. He realised, too, that as a policeman he would have to spend too much of his time causing misery to good people, and was filled with disgust at the meanness of life. So he left the world and became a hermit.

This visit to the hermits in their rock-caves over the sea made an unforgettable impression. I would have liked to visit them all and hear their stories. But we had a very long climb in front of us, if we were to reach Kerassiá that night. So we returned to Katounakia and continued climbing higher into the wilderness of stone and rock, the wildest part of Athos, bare of all vegetation except for occasional thorny shrubs. Low, heavy clouds tore past overhead. It began to grow dark. Far below, grey waves scratched lines across the black sea. The stones slipped under our feet and ran down the slope. Rain began to pour down in large drops. Then all of a sudden we heard a strange irregular knocking. It was impossible to say where it came from; it was strangely threatening. For two hours we had not seen a trace of a human being. The formation of this part of the Mountain is so irregular, and there are so many tiny paths among the bare rocks, each looking exactly like the other, that we were afraid of losing our way. But on mounting a ridge we caught sight of a tiny house half-built, with a dark figure spread across the roof like a great bird, hammering on slates. This was the explanation of the knocking. We asked the way to St Basil's, the next colony of hermits, which turned out to be quite close at hand. A thin rain blew across our faces, but we did not want to spend a night in a primitive *kellion*,* and still hoped to be able to reach Kerassiá, where our luggage and provisions were waiting for us, before the night came on. As we hurried through a wood and small ilex trees and approached the first houses of St Basil's, the rain began to pour again in torrents. A monk standing in a doorway asked us to take shelter in his *kellion*.

It was the most primitive, miserable dwelling imaginable. Three cells opened off a dark narrow corridor: one was a kitchen, another arranged as a carpenter's workshop, and the third was empty. The entrance to a small chapel was at one end of the passage, while at the other end a rickety staircase led to the only 'room' in the building. It was quite small. The furniture consisted of two wooden benches, with coarse coverlets, one chair, and a light tottering table; two cheap pictures of saints and sentimental angels hung on the walls. There were three windows with broken panes. We were offered slices of raw quince, and tin mugs of water, and shown a small carved relief in wood of St George killing the dragon, on which one of the monks had been working for over a month.

It was now dark, and there was no alternative to spending the night in this *kellion*. We went down to the kitchen. A pot was boiling on the fire. There were some shelves on the walls with a few plates, forks and spoons, and in the middle of the room stood a home-made table on which an oil-lamp was burning. Only two monks lived in the house, Kallinikos, a Cretan, and his companion Simeon, an Anatolian from Angora, both young men. Simeon did most of the work. He was short with a long black beard, and had previously earned his living by playing an oriental instrument in the streets of

*A detached cottage for two or three monks.

Athens. In Athos, however, musical instruments are forbidden, and Simeon had now become a wood-carver. It was he who had done the little relief of St George.

At last the food was ready – our first meal that day. But it was not very exciting, consisting only of potato and onion soup, followed by some more raw quince. The bread was so hard and dry that it had to be put in a basin of cold water to soften it; we were thankful still to have some of the loaf of bread the other Father Kallinikos had given us in the morning at St Anne's.

After dinner Simeon went away with a lamp to light the stove upstairs, and we sat in the dark glow coming from the fire. Another monk from some nearby skite came and sat down with us. He also intended to spend the night in the *kellion*, as it was the best and largest in St Basil's.

The conversation started with the assassination of the King of Yugoslavia. As he was king of an Orthodox country, the whole of Mount Athos was very interested in the event. The subject of the calendar was soon brought up. It is a favourite topic everywhere, The usual complaints were made that the Government wanted to throw the monks out of Athos because they insisted on keeping to the old calendar. Vatopèdi is the only monastery which uses the modern European calendar, but in consequence it is despised by all the others, who never send representatives to its feasts.

Then the Cretan, Kallinikos, said to me:

'You know that Germany is going to become Orthodox very soon. The Holy Fathers have prophesied it. It is said that there is now a great king ruling in Germany, who slaughters all the Jews and the Bolsheviks. We love him for that. It is the beginning of the prophecy. But you must go and see Father Ierasimos; he knows all about it.'

Then Simeon came back and asked Kallinikos to help him with the stove. It had not been lit since the previous winter and something had gone wrong. The room was so thick with smoke that one could not even see where the stove was. Finally, after an hour, it began to burn. It was a special honour that the stove should be lit for us, just as the meal we had been given was unusually luxurious for St Basil's.

We lay down on hard benches. It was too cold for bugs. The wind howled round the house all night. When we woke at dawn the sky was still grey and heavy, but the rain had stopped. We drank a small cup of Turkish coffee and thanked Father Kallinikos for his hospitality, for which he would accept nothing.

Before starting off for Kerassiá, we went to visit Father Ierasimos, who lived quite alone in a tiny little house on a cliff. He was an Athenian. Before becoming a monk he had been a chemist, and had studied in Switzerland and Munich and spoke excellent German. Afterwards he had worked for some years in Egypt. When he first came to Athos fifteen years ago, he lived with an older father, down at Katounakia; but when the latter died, he decided to live higher up the Mountain. He had a touch of consumption, and the air up at St Basil's suited him better. His present house was built entirely by his own hands.

Father Ierasimos was comparatively learned, and had quite a respectable theological library in his one-room house. He told us more about the prophecies concerning Germany, and said there was to be a war in the immediate future. It would not last long, but would be the most terrible war that has ever been fought, and would destroy the greater part of Europe. But it would be the last war in the world's history: peace would follow.

It ought not to take more than an hour to go from St Basil's to Kerassiá, which is situated more or less on the same level, about 2,400 feet above the sea; but we lost our way several times along the rocks, and it took us nearly twice as long.

Kerassiá is not a skite, but only a settlement of hermits living in *kellia*, like Katounakia, Karoulia and St Basil's. It is, however, the principal halting place on the main route from St Paul's to Lavra and at the same time the starting point for an ascent of Mount Athos. The Mountain towers above it, but the sea is only visible where the ground drops suddenly between two humps. Although so high up, the aspect of the place was very green; there were some fruit trees and many walnuts. It had a far more prosperous look than the other settlements we had passed on this part of the Mountain. The *kellia* were large, surrounded by well-filled gardens.

Our luggage had been sent to the house of Dorotheus, the Russian, the largest in Kerassiá, and the usual stopping place for travellers. Dorotheus was eighty-three, and came there fifty-seven years ago when there were thirty-three monks in the house; now there are only seven, all aged Russians. He was very tall, with a long, pointed beard. The house had many rooms in good condition and a big chapel filled with gaudy modern Russian pictures of saints. The dining-room was underneath the chapel, with room for a large number of people. For lunch we were given an excellent salad of mixed raw vegetables, and snails, which one sucked through a hole made in the upper end of the shell, prepared with a delicious sauce. Fish and fried potatoes followed and the wine of Kerassiá, famous throughout Athos.

13

Kafsokalyvia – A Colony of Painter-Monks

After a short halt at Kerassiá we got a mule to take our luggage down to Kafsokalyvia. At first the path was fairly level, passing though the vineyards, until it reached the edge of the hump and descended in sharp zigzags down the side of a ravine covered with loose stones, which slipped under one's feet, and with blocks of pale grey rock. Occasionally there were little groves of ilexes, the only trees in this wild gorge which dropped precipitously down to the sea.

After an hour we reached the first houses of Kafsokalyvia. It is an idiorhythmic skite, a dependency of Lavra with at least thirty houses and over 100 monks. It is famous for its painters and wood-carvers, who live in small groups. Laurel oil is also made from the leaves of the trees growing near the lower houses about 150 feet above the sea.

We put up at the house of the Prior (the *dikaios*), built on the steep slope of the mountain. It stood on one side of a large paved terrace in the middle of which grew an immense ilex tree. At the opposite end was the church of the Holy Trinity, its belfry dating probably from the eighteenth century. This church is very similar in plan to the one of St Anne's, except that it is a good deal smaller. Connected with it is a large square room with a dome about twenty feet wide, considerably broader than that of the main church, to which it served as a form of narthex.

The Prior was a genial white-bearded old man, who welcomed us warmly and gave us a comfortable cheerful bedroom with two beds and two couches. The windows opened on to a wooden balcony. On the floor below was a large kitchen where the Prior told us stories for hours on end. Two other younger monks who did the manual work were all living in the house.

We had a very pleasant time during our four days' stay with the Prior. The food was good and Iorgos made himself agreeable and became chief cook; he started a competition with the Prior, each cooking a dish of his own. The other monks and I had to decide which was best.

We spent the greater part of our days paying visits, and the first person we went to see was our painter friend, Chrysostomos, the young deacon whom we had met at the feast at Xiropotamou. He was living in a sizeable house, unusually neat-looking for this part of the world, and lying in a charming garden, a little farther down the slope from the Prior's. It included an elaborately decorated chapel and, on the first floor, a big studio. Chrysostomos lived with his younger brother, aged sixteen, and the Ierondas, the master, an old grey-bearded monk. But the charming young deacon was by far the most vital member of the household, known and liked by everyone in the whole neighbourhood. They were all natives of Crete and sent most of the sacred images they painted there.

The work done here, as everywhere else at Kafsokalyvia, is very second-rate and consists mainly in copying. The monks have a number of photographs of modern Russian icons which are much admired, and which they copy on a large scale on wood, varying the colour of the drapery according to their fancy. There is no original work done. At the most they have a certain series of possibilities, six different heads of saints, six bodies with the hands in varying positions, and three or four colour schemes. They combine these units in various ways, but that is the limit of their invention.

It is the custom in those studios and workshops for one monk to make the drawing, another to put on the first coat, another the second, while the Ierondas himself usually adds the finishing touches. Very often he, too, makes the original drawing.

Chrysostomos was twenty-two. He told me he had been brought to Athos by the Ierondas when he was only twelve, and so had become a monk without ever having any real choice in the matter. In spite of various difficulties, he seemed to be fairly satisfied with his life, and certainly managed to be marvellously cheerful and lively. He did, however, very strongly criticise the kind of work that was done and found the gold discs put round the heads of saints horrible. He would prefer to paint realistically, using natural colours, with at the most a thin gold circle round the saints' heads. But unfortunately the market demands that these pictures be painted according to a conventional pattern, and if the monks were to do anything else, they would find few buyers.

'The old women who buy our pictures like a lot of gold,' said

Chrysostomos. 'It is horrible. And then they go and cover up most of them with plates of wrought silver. A number of my pictures have been utterly ruined that way by foolish old women. But there is nothing to be done: it is the custom.'

Perhaps the largest and best known of the houses in Kafsokalyvia is the one called after the painter Josaphat. Its fame has spread all over the Mountain. In all seven monks live in it, the youngest being a novice only twelve years old. A long wooden veranda runs along the first floor outside the studio, overhung with the fat dark green leaves of a creeper which twists interminably backwards and forwards. The walls of the reception room and veranda are covered with bad-taste photographs, including four enormous ones of girls draped in pseudo-ancient Greek costumes either playing lutes or sitting on marble seats with pigeons on their laps. In the studio were some large pictures, painted late in the nineteenth century by Father Josaphat, the founder of the house, representing Christ and the Virgin on carved wooden thrones typical of the heavy furniture of that period. The Ierondas told us that when the monks were in search of a theme for their next picture they looked up and found inspiration in these works of Josaphat. Here, too, most of the pictures of saints were done from photographs, originality being confined to the invention of the colour of the drapery. St George and St Nicholas were the favourite subjects.

All the monks at Kafsokalyvia are artists of one kind or another. Several of them are wood-carvers. The doyen of these is Father Arsenios, who has been thirty-seven years on the Holy Mountain. We found him living in a pleasantly situated house among olives and oleanders, ilex and medlar trees, together with three other monks – all, like himself, natives of Smyrna. The interior of the house was quite Turkish, with a long couch running right across the wall under the windows, on which the monks reclined even when working on carvings. Father Arsenios showed us photographs of two large complicated carvings of the Crucifixion and the Last Judgment, in very high relief, which he had recently sold for a good price to America.

I had been struck by a landscape drawing of the monastery of Vatopèdi hanging in our room at the Prior's. It interested me as being totally different from any other work I had seen on Athos. The Prior told me it was by a Father Niphon, one of the monks of Kafsokalyvia; so I went and looked for him. He lived much lower down, quite alone, in a little two-roomed house with a courtyard. He worked only in black and white, doing mainly portraits of Emperors such as Nicephorus Phocas and John Tzimiskes and elders of the Church, besides a few landscapes. But his work, too, was mainly from photographs. As a young man he had always wanted to be an artist, and when he had saved a little money he went to a college of art in Athens; but after a very short time his money was exhausted, and he was left penniless. He heard somehow of Kafsokalyvia as being a good place for an artist to work, and so came to Athos. But he was now rather disappointed and found it very hard to make a living. Nor did his work please him. But when I suggested he might try for a change to do some drawing from Nature, he was quite astonished and considered it was a very hazardous experiment, quite against all custom. Still, he asked me to send him photographs of works of art which I admired to see if they would give him new inspiration.

I was surprised to find him living alone, and asked him if he had never had anyone with him. Father Niphon said he had, and began to tell a long story with such interest and wealth of detail that he clearly considered it the most exciting thing that had ever happened to him.

'Petros came here from Lavra,' he said. 'He was not satisfied with the life there and told me he hoped to find peace in a skite. He asked me to let him live with me as a novice. I was struck by his delicate features and well-kept appearance, showing he came from a well-to-do family. And the fact was confirmed by a few remarks he made about his past life. I was rather worried as to whether he could really stand the severe hard life we led, particularly as I felt he wished to become a monk rather as a result of some tragedy in his life than as a real vocation. But whenever I asked him questions about himself and his life he shut himself up completely, and said nothing. He used to sleep on the floor in the other cell, but often he didn't lie down at all, and kept walking up and down his room or in the courtyard all night long. One night, however, after he had been working all day on the roof, which had been damaged by a storm, I heard him shouting to himself in his sleep: "Koula, Koula, why did you abandon me? Why did you leave me?" Next morning I said to him: "You spoke of Koula in your sleep. You have been with me now for a long time, why is it you never told me of her?"

'He was silent for a while, then he answered: "When I was in the world I loved a girl called Koula Nikolaidis. She was the most beautiful and admired girl in Salonica, and of very good family. My father was rich, and I asked him to give me money to start a business of my own, as I wanted to marry. But he was a miser, and took no interest in my plans, saying: 'When you are older and can take business seriously I may give you money for that, and also for marrying.' I had never spoken to him about the girl I loved, so I suppose he didn't realise what a blow he was giving me in putting things off like that."

'I asked Petros', went on Father Niphon, 'if he really loved Koula so much then.

' "Yes, indeed," he said, "who could have helped loving her? She had promised to marry me, and I thought she loved me, too. Every day we met at the Church of St Demetrius, so that no one should observe us, and then we walked through the old Turkish quarter of the town, up the hill to the fortress. One day Koula said to me: 'Things cannot go on like this, we must marry at once.' I explained to her that my father did not want me to marry yet, and would give me no money. I beseeched her to be patient and wait another two years. But Koula was upset, and seemed to think I was only putting off marrying her because I didn't really love her.

' "From that day she began to come and meet me more rarely, and finally one evening she said: 'You know, my father is going to engage me to Andreas Pirounakis' – a well-known business man. 'It is better that we should not see each other any more, and that things should come to an end between us without any quarrel.'

' "Three days later I read the announcement of her engagement in the newspaper, and the same evening I decided to come to Athos and become a monk, without telling a soul about it.

' "I went at first to the monastery of Iviron, then to Karakallou, Philotheou, and Lavra. But I cold not forget Koula and find the peace I was looking for. At Lavra I was told: 'If you are seeking still greater peace, go to a skite, go to Kafsokalyvia.' And so I came here to you."

'That was the story Petros told me; but in the meantime his father, as I learned later, was in despair at his son's disappearance. He went to every acquaintance to see if they knew anything. He informed the police, but not a trace was to be found. At last someone told him by chance that Petros had loved Koula Nikolaidis, the well-known beauty in Salonica society, who was in a few days to marry Andreas Pirounakis. The father went at once to the Nikolaidises' house, and asked to see Koula. He told her all that had happened and said: "I have lost my son, can you help me to find him?" Koula asked on what day Petros had disappeared, and when she heard that it was the same day as the announcement of her engagement, she was filled with a dreadful remorse, realising what a mistake she had made not to believe in the reality of Petros's love for her. Then she remembered some words of his one evening when they had sat together on the ruined walls of the fortress looking over the Gulf towards Olympus. Petros had clasped her hands and cried: "If you don't marry me, Koula, I shall either kill myself or become a monk." She began to weep, and said to Petros's father, "If he's still alive, he must be on Mount Athos."

'So the father hired a yacht and sailed off with Koula, who had broken off her engagement to Andreas, for the Holy Mountain. They anchored in front of each monastery, and while poor Koula waited on board, her heart racing, the father visited the monks, describing his son and asking if they had heard of anyone like him. But at monastery after monastery he had no success, and began to fear his son must be dead. At last the yacht came to Lavra, and here he learned that a couple of months before a young man had come, but had left and gone to Kafsokalyvia.

'The yacht anchored down there, beside those rocks,' said Niphon, pointing. 'The father came up and made inquiries at each house. He was told that two young men had recently come. One was with Father Arsenios, the other with me. First he went to Father Arsenios's, but the young novice there was not his son.

'Then he came to my little house, and as he entered the court, he saw Petros sweeping the floor. I was in here drawing, when I suddenly heard the old man's voice crying: "Ah, my son, my son, there you are!" I rushed out and saw my novice in his father's arms, both unable to restrain their tears. The old man said: "Petros, my son, how could you run away from your old father like that? Koula is waiting for you in the yacht."

'I was deeply moved, listening to this, and said to Petros: "You are only a novice, you can still choose your route in life. Do you want to remain on the Holy Mountain, or do you want to return to the world?"

'Petros took off his cassock, and we went all three down to the yacht. Koula was even more beautiful than I had imagined, and when I saw her and Petros in each other's arms I understood.

'That night they sailed away happily, and a fortnight later I received a letter from Petros to tell me he was married.'

Niphon seemed very moved by his own story.

'Yes my boy, one must realise what one is giving up when one comes to live on the Holy Mountain,' he said. 'It is hard.'

After dinner that evening I told the Prior about Niphon's story. He knew about it already, of course, and said that a somewhat similar experience had happened once to himself. I was very curious and asked him to tell me the story.

'Some years ago,' he began, 'I had a young deacon called Pannos staying with me. He was the most silent man I had ever met, and though he had been staying with me for several months I had never been able to get anything out of him about himself. His face never showed any emotion but I could see that he had some great weight on his conscience.

'It was winter, the snow had been falling for two days, and we were compelled to remain indoors all the time, sitting bedside the fire in the kitchen. His silence and gloom began to communicate themselves to me, and I felt that something must be done. So I said to him: "Today you must open your heart to me, tomorrow you can confess to God!" It is an expression we have in Greek, you know. He replied: "I am guilty in the eyes of the world, and you will condemn me for what I have done; but God will forgive me as I have repented." I insisted, however, that he should tell me his story, which he finally did.

'"As you know," said Pannos, "I come from he island of Hydra. Like a good many other men there, I was a sponge-diver. I loved a girl called Nausicaa, the daughter of a doctor. Her beauty was extraordinary, and many men wanted to marry her. But she loved me and refused them all, although her father tried to forbid her to see me and make her marry someone rich. We were wildly happy together, and I hoped to be able to save up enough money to start a business of my own, so that I could simply take her away from her father. But the sponge-diving season varies, and sometimes I had to leave Hydra for months on end. At last I thought I had enough money to bring my dreams to fulfilment. I had been diving off the North African coast and returned to Hydra eager to tell Nausicaa of my plans.

'"As soon as I landed I began to inquire from my friends how Nausicaa was. But they all replied very vaguely and it seemed to me that something must be wrong. At last I learned that she spent all her time with a rich young man from Athens, who had come to Hydra for the summer. I was struck with terror and searched everywhere for her. I visited her house. I asked everyone I met. But no one could tell me where she was. Finally a child told me that he had seen her with a man on a road leading out of the town. It was growing dark. I ran like a madman across the fields and among the trees, which looked huge and mysterious in the light of the stars. Not a leaf moved: the silence was so heavy that I thought I would choke. And then, under an old olive tree, I saw them entwined in each other's arms. I roared with despair and rage and rushed forward, my knife in my hand. The man jumped up and ran away, vanishing in the darkness. I paid no attention to him. Nausicaa did not stir. There was no terror in her face. She looked straight at me with her big eyes. But I drove my knife into her breast. As her eyes closed she whispered my name. I stood and watched a thread of blood run across her skin. She had never looked more beautiful; I began to weep.

' "Then I made my way down to the water, took a small boat, and rowed over to the mainland of Argolis. All next day I walked, till I reached Mehana, where I found a caique to take me to Athens. I felt quite broken with remorse at what I had done in killing Nausicaa, whom I loved, and came here to Mount Athos."

'While Pannos was telling me his story an idea occurred to me, and I asked him if he had a photograph of the girl. He said he had. I begged him to let me see it, and he brought it from his room. I remembered having read a story similar to his in a newspaper that someone had happened to leave with me a few months before. I still had it, and went to fetch it. A newspaper is something rather rare with us, you know,' said the Prior, and smiled. 'There was a photograph of the girl in the paper with an account of the tragic event, and I saw at once that it was the same. I came running back to Pannos, and cried: "You didn't kill Nausicaa, you only wounded her. She's not dead. Look at this paper."

'Pannos saw that it was Nausicaa, but did not say a word.

'The snow continued for another two days. Then the sun came out. Pannos said to me, "Ierondas, I will go and cut some wood", and went out after taking off his over-gown, as monks usually do when they have some work to carry out.

'I waited all day for him, but he did not return. At first I thought he might be staying at some other *kellion*, as the weather was bad again. But a month passed, without any news from him: he had simply disappeared. Then a letter came for me one morning. It contained a photograph of Pannos and Nausicaa seated side by side smiling.'

[90]

14

Grand Lavra

We had intended to do the last part of the journey to Lavra by sea. But it was still rather stormy, and there was no sign of any boat coming. This might have been awkward as there were no mules to be had at the skite. By chance, however, a monk, Father Basil, came down from Kerassiá one day with several mule-loads of supplies and we tried to arrange with him that he should take us and our luggage. His prices were enormous, but we were compelled to come to an agreement with him. He was to take our luggage up to Kerassiá, where we would follow an hour or two later, and decide definitely whether we should take mules for ourselves, or only for our luggage. When we arrived at Father Basil's house, quite a large building where he lived with a young novice and a puppy, the tariff of prices had made a jump. Father Basil evidently thought he could take advantage of our situation to ask exactly double his former exorbitant demands. So we arranged a price for the luggage which was to be brought along to Lavra the following morning, and decided ourselves to go on foot. When Father Basil did arrive at Lavra, his price had made a further upward jump, and we had to call in the policeman who is stationed at Lavra to help us, finally splitting the difference to get rid of the man. It was the first time we had ever had such an experience on Athos, but no one at Lavra was surprised at it. Father Basil has the worst character on the Mountain, and has been in prison a number of times. He is summoned to court every few months. A monk told us laughingly the nickname by which he is known all over Athos, which meant 'Basil the Liar'.

To the east of Kerassiá, about ten minutes' walk from the house of Dorotheus, is a large fountain where mules come to drink and a number of paths cross each other. Two of them continue to the east, the upper one leading to Lavra, the lower to Kafsokalyvia. We now took the Lavra road, one of the pleasantest walks on the Mountain – a continuous gentle descent of a little over two hours, passing through some of the finest parts of Athos.

The sun was shining from a clear sky that afternoon, as we walked past the fountain. It was the finest day there had been for two weeks. The bushes and shrubs beside the path became larger and larger as we went, until after about a quarter of an hour we found ourselves in a real forest of immense oaks, chestnuts and beech trees covered with ivy, and great clumps of prickly holly with scarlet berries. The trees here have never been cut down as in most other parts of the Mountain, where the wood is sold as soon as it grows up. Above us, beyond the forest, shining walls of rock towered up one above the other, and below one could see through the trees further precipices dropping down to the sea. The forest is just a broad belt between the bare faces of rock, where chamois and jackals live undisturbed.

After about an hour the path turned a corner and a new world opened in front of us. No more white cliffs tumbling down to the sea, but a soft pasture country, stretching away in dark green waves to the deep sea beyond. To the right was a large complex of buildings, two or three miles away, near the water, looking like a monastery. It was the 'Prodrom', the Rumanian skite of St John the Baptist. The Rumanians have no monastery of their own, and hoped to get the 'Prodrom' recognised as one; but they failed, and it remains a coenobian skite, dependent on Lavra, containing fifty-four monks. In form the buildings seemed to be like those of a monastery, and from a distance looked quite picturesque in their green setting. But when we came closer we saw that they were dull and modern. As we were in a hurry to reach Lavra before the gates were shut, we kept to our path.

After so many days spent on the uncanny precipitous slopes of Mount Athos, following tracks often mere ledges cut in the cliff face, it was an extraordinary relief not to be shut in any more, to be able to breathe freely in an open landscape. There was a fresh evening breeze. The little bells of black and white rams and he-goats tinkled around us on every side.

For about an hour the path remained open, then entered another belt of great oaks and chestnuts. In front, towards the north-west, one could make out in the distance through the trees towers and high walls. It was getting late, and we began to run faster and faster until we suddenly saw a town in front of us, a real, small town, with wide-spreading walls and roofs, towers and cupolas. This was 'Grand Lavra', far exceeding all expectations. This was how a town looked in the Middle Ages. But then we were living in the Middle Ages. It was forty days since we had had any contact with the modern world, and we had almost forgotten it. We were in the Byzantine Empire. The magnificent, rather squat tower, rising to the left of the monastery and built by the Emperor John Tzimiskes, was a symbol of strength, such as exists nowhere else on the Holy Mountain. Chilandari, Dochiariou, Stavronikita and Dionysiou have their towers, some higher, some more graceful, but none of them rivals the massive beauty of the tower of Tzimiskes. Its simplicity and majesty express an earlier epoch of Byzantine civilisation. It was built in A.D. 970, and is the oldest building existing on Mount Athos.

We halted for a moment at a peasant house beside the walls to drink from a fountain, and then walked round to the gateway to the north-west corner, in front of which was a modern porch similar to that at Vatopèdi. The porter came out of his little shop where he sold cigarettes, tinned provisions, rosaries, and so on, and took our letters of recommendation. We passed through three successive gates, which were about be locked for the night, and entered a small square. This was only part of the immense court, filled with buildings of every kind. Here at Lavra one really had the impression of being in a little town. Passing through a kind of street, with a chapel on one side and the guest house on the other, we reached another open space between the main church and the refectory. And here grew two monumental cypresses, planted 1,000 years ago by St Athanasius, the founder of the monastery.

Father Ierasimos, of St Basil's, had told us that we must be sure to visit Father Athanasius, one of the epitropes (members of the Administrative Council), as he was best fitted to show us the treasury and the library (of which he had made a catalogue). He had an apartment of three of four rooms at the south-east end of the court, painted blue outside, with a terrace overlooking the sea hung with tomatoes and onions. We were ushered by an attendant monk into a rather disorderly room: a good many books were lying about and portraits of John Tzimiskes, Nicephorus Phocas and St Athanasius by Niphon of Kafsokalyvia hung on the walls. Father Athanasius was dressed in rustling silk, a decoration on his dress – the typical figure of a dignified ecclesiastic, with a 'man of the world' manner. He received us with great politeness and ceremony, and asked us to return the following morning after the service, that is at 6 a.m., as if he were inviting us to a banquet. We saw him on a number of occasions, and learned his story.

[93]

He had studied medicine at the University of Athens, where he had one particular friend to whom he was most closely attached. In 1893 he began his military service and was separated from his friend for a period of two years. When he returned he found everything altered. His own three sisters had all married, and he found it impossible to recover the old terms of intimacy with his friend, who had anyway made up his mind to go to America. Athanasius found himself alone. The study of religion engrossed him more and more; he spent his whole time reading religious books. And one day he came to a decision, and said to his mother:

'I am going to Mount Athos to become a monk.'

She replied: 'If you believe that you can, and have the inner strength to serve God and not mankind, then go.'

He settled at Lavra, where his medical knowledge was made use of. After some years he happened to be called in to attend the Patriarch Joachim, who was on a visit to the Mountain. The Patriarch offered to send him to Constantinople to study further. He agreed and stopped a few days on the way at Piraeus to visit his mother. While he was there a telegram came from the monastery, asking him to return immediately. He said to himself, however: 'I won't go, there are other doctors on Athos.' But three days later a second telegram arrived. His mother advised him to go and see what he was wanted for, and then to go on to Constantinople.

On arriving at the monastery he found fifteen monks ill with plague. He was not allowed to order the necessary medicines from Athens, as it would then have become publicly known that there was plague on the Mountain and the monastery would have been closed. So the sick men were put in the charnel house, and Athanasius did what he could with the remedies at his disposal. Half the patients died. When the rest had recovered, however, Athanasius did not continue his journey to Constantinople. He felt that just as God had called him to the Holy Mountain the first time, so God had called him back again and that it was not His will that he should leave.

15

Deacon Niphon of Lavra

Although Lavra has more mules than any monastery, we had severe difficulties in getting one to carry our things to the next monastery: apparently all fifty were required for the olive harvest. One afternoon a young dandy from Athens, called Simon, came up to us in the courtyard. He seemed to know a great many people in the monastery.

'Mules?' he said. 'Did you say they refused you mules? Leave that to me. If I ask the Epitropes for them, you'll get as many as you want, whenever you want.' He was boasting of course.

It was not Simon's first visit; he was employed in a mysterious capacity by an Armenian who annually buys quantities of wood from the Lavra forests, which is shipped in caiques to Athens. Simon was a highly unsympathetic person, always dressed most elegantly, while Andreas, the Armenian, who was small and oily and good-natured, looked like a common workman.

I had little hope of Simon being able to help us about the mules, but was glad of the opportunity to visit the Epitrope's office, as I had been told by Dr L–, who had visited Lavra a couple of years before, that he was convinced the under-secretary there was really a woman in disguise. I was anxious to investigate the facts.

The office was a large room with an altar in one corner; a sacred lamp burned in front of an image of the Virgin. In the other corner was a safe from which a monk was handing out money to a peasant. Elaborate refreshments were served on a huge tray, but I was disappointed as the secretary was old, with a long beard, and clearly not a woman. I found out, however, that the year Dr L– visited the monastery someone else had had his place. We thanked the Epitrope for the drinks he had given us, and went with Simon to see Father Eulogios, the chief secretary, with whom he was staying. He was a gentle old man, learned and full of charm, with an extensive library.

Simon then dragged us off through long, dark corridors to the apartment of his friend Deacon Niphon, whom we found drinking *râki* with Andreas, the Armenian. They were both a little tipsy already, and insisted on our sitting down and drinking with them. Iorgos and I had had enough *râki* that day, and in any case we didn't care for it very much, so we were given tumblerfuls of red wine. Meanwhile Simon had been trying to open a tin of sardines. The key broke; so he had a shot with a kitchen knife. That was no good either, so he fetched a hefty pair of pincers from the workshop on the ground floor. Even that was unsuccessful.

'Give it to me,' said Andreas, half drunk, and set to work on the box with the pincers. Then the Deacon fetched another knife, and all three of them hacked and hammered at the poor tin, until it suddenly burst and squirted oil everywhere. The Deacon, who was big and fat, sat back in his chair, sweating after his efforts. His little glittering eyes almost vanished with amusement, and a wide, dog-like grin spread over his face. Simon rescued what he could of the sardines and spread them on bits of bread which he enthusiastically offered to everyone.

'Tell us a story, Deacon Niphon,' asked Andreas.

'I'll give you a riddle,' he replied, and began: 'I am queen of the highest mountains and the loveliest valleys; I devour the flesh of human beings. But when I fall from my mountain tops, I'm captured, and crushed between two cliffs.'

'The louse,' said Iorgos.

'Bravo,' said the Deacon. 'Now I'll ask you another riddle.'

He asked three more. I began to be bored. It showed, I suppose, in my expression.

'Just look at him,' said Simon, pointing to me. 'He's worried.'

'Cheer up, my boy, cheer up,' said the Deacon.

I tried to protest that I was perfectly cheerful, but Simon broke in, and said:

'You know, he has every reason for his worry.'

I began to be embarrassed.

'What's the matter? What has happened?' asked Niphon. Simon winked to me to be quiet, and said, his voice dropping to a whisper:

'Listen, Deacon, we will tell you a great secret if you can keep quiet about it.'

'Go on, go on,' said Father Niphon, 'whatever you tell me will remain locked up in my heart. You can tell me anything.' His face became quite serious, and his big body jerked about in his chair with eagerness and curiosity.

'Well,' said Simon, 'one of the Epitropes of Vatopèdi has given these fellows a lot of money for them to bring him a woman, secretly, to the monastery.'

I was astonished to hear this amazing story, but was interested to see what effect it would have. Simon went on:

'They have brought her along in a caique. She is down at Father Onophrio's cell, near the Arsenal, and they have given him money so that he should make her a monk immediately. He's busy teaching her prayers. But it is necessary to get her quickly to Vatopèdi before Father Onophrios finds out that she is a girl.'

Deacon Niphon found the matter of absorbing interest.

'She's dressed as a man, of course?' he asked. 'Well, well,' turning to me, 'don't be worried. Everything can be arranged. I'll notify Pholia tomorrow. He runs a motor-boat along the coast. We'll put her on board and take a lot of *râki* with us, and as soon as we have started, we'll give Pholia so much to drink that he won't notice anything. Just let me know which day you want the boat.'

'That's very good of you,' said Simon. 'So you will help us?'

'Of course I will,' replied Father Niphon, 'but take care. Some time ago a monk who had a motor-boat brought some women to Athos. He was caught and kicked out. I don't want that to happen to me. Still, I'll help you with her.'

That matter was settled by drinking a round of *râki*, and it was decided that Iorgos and I should not go back to the guest-house for dinner, where the food was scandalously bad and we should only have bean soup and bread, but that we should all stay and dine with the Deacon.

Simon was sent to collect things to eat.

'When you come to Piraeus,' said the Armenian to Niphon, 'you must come and stay with me.'

'Fine,' said the Deacon. 'But see that no such ridiculous adventure happens to me as happened to one monk. Let me tell you.' As the story went on, it became quite clear that it was really Niphon himself who had had the adventure.

'Well, then, a monk went once to Athens to meet a friend, like you for example. In the evening they went out together to an eating-house to amuse themselves, and seeing that we monks are rather fond of wine, as you are well aware, they drank one glass after another, till they were both rather drunk. Then the monk asked his friend to accompany him back to his hotel, as he didn't know his way about Athens very well. The friend, however, brought him instead to one of

[97]

those houses which have a small red lantern hanging outside. But the monk didn't notice anything, and went straight inside. Somehow he got separated from his friend, and set out to look for his bedroom. One of the women came up to him and said: "Come along, I'll show you your room", and he, without suspecting anything, followed her into a dark room, where she began to caress him. The monk told her she could go away now, and she said:

'"What, you want to *sleep* the whole night, darling?"

'"Of course, the same as every night."

'"Ah, but on other nights you haven't been with me; you must have gone to someone else, you naughty monk."

'What followed he couldn't remember, but after some time he was awakened by a scream, and heard a hoarse, woman's voice in the next room, making a row because she hadn't received the money she was expecting. Then the monk realised for the first time to what kind of place he had come to spend the night.'

The Deacon now dropped all pretence, and went on in the first person.

'I was thunderstruck at the discovery, jumped up and tried to run out of the house. But a woman, whose face seemed in some way familiar, grasped my arm, and cried:

'"Father, Father, how can you think of going away, when you haven't paid me for my visit?"

'When the other women heard these words, they made a circle round me, pointing and screaming:

'"Look, look, we've got a monk here, a monk. Bah! Bah! Bah!"

'I pulled some money from my pocket and rushed through the door into the dark street. It had been raining, and I stumbled and fell into a puddle. I had no idea where I was and it was half an hour before I found my hotel. And then I was obliged to lie to the hotel-keeper to explain why I was all covered with mud.

'So you see,' concluded the Deacon, ' I shouldn't like anything like that to happen to me again if I go to Athens,'

'Ah, Father Niphon,' said Andreas, 'if we go somewhere drinking together, I certainly shan't take you to a house with a red lantern afterwards. The best ones have no lanterns at all!'

As the Deacon gave his dog-like grin and refilled our wine glasses, Simon came back with the food, various miscellaneous remnants of meals. There was a plate of cold snails in a yellow sauce, a salad of tomatoes and onions, lots of Greek goat-cheese, nuts, an enormous mushroom the size of a soup-plate cooked in a delicious sauce, and three eggs. The Deacon, Iorgos and Simon went into the kitchen to fry the eggs. Meanwhile Andreas began to take bits of the mushroom, and offered some to me. By the time the others came back there was none left. The meal, however, went off quite well.

Then Andreas, who had taken too much wine, began to made a dreadful noise. He was trying to sing an oriental song, but was too drunk to succeed. The Deacon tried to restrain him.

'Quiet, quiet. If the Archimandrite, who sleeps upstairs, hears singing, he'll make a scene tomorrow. I'll show you how one sings in a monastery.'

He drank another glass of wine and began to sing in a soft, high voice a typical oriental song about dark eyes and dark wine. We had to keep time by beating our glasses on the table.

'Now that was a fine song!' he concluded, looking round triumphantly. Andreas obviously considered it was his turn now and began again until Niphon stopped him with the threat of a riddle. No one, however, wanted to hear riddles. Iorgos and Simon had been whispering together, and now said they wanted to go to bed.

'No, no,' said the Deacon. 'I'll show you something. Who'll take on a bet? I will balance a match on the edge of a wine glass, and then on the match I will balance two forks.'

'Impossible!' we said.

Simon bet a thousand drachmas against it; but the Deacon said:

'No, I don't want you to have to pay me a thousand drachmas. I'll show you how it's done and then you can bet with other people.'

He performed the feat, to everyone's astonishment.

At last we stood up to go to bed, but the result was that everyone came to my room and wanted to sleep there. They were all quite drunk. Andreas still wanted to sing. Iorgos and Simon lay with their arms round each other on my bed. Niphon grinned. It took me half an hour to get rid of them all.

Whenever one saw Deacon Niphon, he seemed to be drinking or feasting. He always found an opportunity. On the following day Andreas gave a party at a farmhouse belonging to the monastery, a few minutes' walk up the hill. Niphon and one or two other monks were there, as well as Simon. The house was quite pretty, with, of course, a chapel and various balconies and verandas. We arrived in the afternoon and found Niphon and Andreas hard at work cracking nuts and drinking *râki*. Somehow or other the Armenian had got hold of a chicken and a rabbit; so everyone shared in the cooking and helped prepare elaborate sauces while the Deacon made tipsy jokes the whole time and sang snatches of songs, such as 'In the nun's cell . . .' etc.

The next day I went down to the harbour which is fortified with a tower at the entrance, unfortunately rebuilt in concrete. A number of peasants and monks were taking a rest from the olive harvest and were picnicking together beside the sea. Deacon Niphon, though scarcely one of the olive-pickers, was, it is hardly necessary to mention, among them. He joined me and we climbed up the rough path back to the monastery together.

On the way I slipped and tore open my hand on the rock. I was at once taken to the doctor to have it dressed. He was a very serious, refined-looking individual, immensely thin, with a white face and a pointed black beard. Over his cassock he wore a long black sleeveless coat, lined and trimmed on the outside with fur. In spite of it he always gave the impression of suffering from cold, and his exquisitely manicured hands were damp and icy. He was unnaturally silent. Hot water was brought in a broken tin can. The doctor simply looked at it and said: 'Not clean.' The tin of hot water was brought back. Again, 'Not clean.' The third time, apparently, the demands of ritual were fulfilled and the water, which seemed the same as before, was accepted. The doctor, though very gentle, was so sinister-looking that I was glad to escape so lightly. I had expected it would be at least necessary to apply the entrails of a rat or something of the kind to the wound.

Deacon Niphon came and had dinner with me in my room, where plenty of wine had been provided. He told me about his early years on Athos, where he had been brought from the island of Samos as quite a child, and about his life with the Ierondas who adopted him. And whom he insisted on referring to as the 'Thavolo-papás' (the Devil Father).

It occurred to me that Niphon would be sure to know the truth about the famous under-secretary who was supposed to be a woman.

'No, no,' he said, 'you should see him now, he's at the Hierarchical College at Karyes, and has a beard two feet long. He was brought here young, I don't suppose he was fifteen. It is true he was very beautiful – but now he is spoiled. By the way, his great friend is still here; they were born in the same village in Crete, and came here about the same time. They even had the same Ierondas.'

Later I made a point of seeing the friend. He told me he came to

Lavra as an inexperienced boy of fourteen. A common acquaintance was sent back to Crete to persuade the boy to become a monk, and described the life on Mount Athos in such attractive terms that the boy left his home and came to Lavra where the Ierondas adopted him. He was now twenty-five years old and in no way disillusioned. In fact he tried to persuade me to become a monk, telling me what a marvellous time I should have, and saying that he had never had any reason to regret his choice.

But to return to Niphon, who was in a particularly confidential mood that evening. He began to tell me his experiences on the island of Skyros, where he had been sent for a few years after the war to look after one of the estates owned there by Lavra.

'Another monk shared the work with me,' he said. 'We had a house for ourselves; there was very little to do, and things went very smoothly till one day we took into the house a servant woman, a refugee from Smyrna called Maria. At first things were all right; but after she had been with us a little while, she insisted on her daughter coming to live in the house too. We agreed, and expected a small child to arrive, instead of which, to our astonishment, a young girl of sixteen or seventeen, with full breasts, turned up. She was very pretty, and we were both very impressed and excited.' The Deacon looked at me out of the corner of his little eyes.

'She was called Helen, and her mother had evidently taught her how to handle monks, or possibly she didn't need any teaching. One little game of hers was to take a stick and poke our bodies with it. We crossed ourselves and cried that the Devil had sent her. But it was only the beginning; she soon became more daring. I forgot myself, and caught hold of her, and tried to embrace her. She began screaming like mad and escaped. What could I do then?' said the Deacon, grinning.

'After that Maria and her daughter began to steal our food and belongings. They had been sent by the Devil, there is no doubt. Just listen to this:

'One day I was in bed with a bad cold, and Maria offered to cup me, promising that next day my cold would be gone. So she took the glass and cupped my back, afterwards rubbing it vigorously. Then she made me turn over and began rubbing my front. I couldn't stand it. I jumped up and shouted: "Leave me alone. You've been sent by Satan." She was frightened and ran away. You see, my boy, what trials we have to suffer?

'Next day Maria brought her daughter into the living-room, where

I was sitting with my colleague, and started making a dreadful scene, complaining that her daughter had pimples on her body. Without a moment's hesitation, she started undressing the girl, until, to our amazement, Helen stood stark naked in front of us. She wasn't the least bit embarrassed either. We were terribly excited. We had never seen anything like it before, you know. It was simply staggering. It was enough to make one mad. And then the mother began to scream hysterically: "My poor daughter, my poor little Helen. What has happened to her? Just look at those pimples all over her body. No, no, it is too dreadful! Who knows what they are? And who is responsible for all this?" She looked at us reproachfully. How can one understand what women want? We turned our heads away and shouted: "Take her away, we will give you medicine, but take her away." At last they left us.

'Shortly afterwards Helen came up alone to my room, and insisted on demonstrating that the pimples had all gone. Then she started playing about with me and pulling my beard. Well, this time there was no resisting. After all, I'm a human being! I caught hold of her, kissed her, and carried her over to the bed. She tried to pretend she didn't want me, the sow, but I took her . . .' Deacon Niphon paused a moment, and then added contemptuously, 'And afterwards I paid her.'

'Oh, my boy, you have no idea at all what trouble we had with those women. It was dreadful. One day there was a "Paniyiris"* on Skyros, and we two monks had decided to go to the feast, to see the dancing. We told Maria and Helen to stay at home, but they became quite wild with fury.

' "We?" they cried. "Do you think we came to this farm to be locked up? We want to enjoy ourselves! We are going to the feast! We come from Smyrna, and we want to amuse ourselves!"

'So in the end we had to stay at home, while the two women went off. But we decided to get rid of them. Oh, if only you knew what we heard about them the next day! Do you know what they had done? Orgies, my boy, orgies! That's how they feasted. Sins, my boy, sins! As soon as they appeared, we told them to pack up their things and clear out. Maria screamed with rage:

"What, you want to kick me out?" she cried. "I will make you pay forty thousand drachmas, do you hear? I will tell what you did with me, and what you did with my daughter." I ran to catch hold of her,'

*Feast of the local patron saint.

said Niphon, with a sigh. 'And if I had succeeded I should have torn out her hair. She screamed that she was going to run into the street and shout the facts so loud that the whole of Skyros would hear it.

'Ah, my boy, if St George hadn't helped me at that moment, the whole town would have heard the lies of that female. But as she rushed downstairs to the street, she fell and wrenched her leg, and lay there helpless. We shut down the farm house and left Skyros by the first steamer.'

The Deacon paused a moment, and then said:

'You see, my boy, they weren't clever enough to catch us, these women. If they had been, they could have taken everything from us, even our cassocks.'

'Hm, yes; and the mother, you didn't do anything there?'

'No. You see, I am a bit of a coward. She didn't make things clear enough.'

16

Karakallou and Philotheou

The ride from Lavra to Karakallou took us between four and five
hours, along a path more or less following the coast towards the
north, continually climbing and descending a series of ridges, the
spurs of the mountain. The whole way was wooded, though the trees
were mostly small, and every few hundred yards we crossed a spring
or a torrent running over mossy stones under plane trees.

About half-way we were struck by the sight of a ruined medieval
tower rising all alone on the summit of a small hill in the centre of a
wild forest-covered valley. This is all that remains of a Latin monastery of Orthodox monks from Amalfi, about whom unfortunately
very little is known.*

Karakallou lies a little inland, but before reaching it one passes the
Arsenal, a crenellated Gothic tower by the sea, built in the sixteenth
century.

After riding through meadows and olive groves we came upon the
tower of the monastery, our third tower that day. It is a magnificent
construction, the highest on Mount Athos, rising above the centre of
the main façade of the building. In this respect it gains immensely in
effect, the towers of other monasteries being either built in corners or
at the back where the ground slopes uphill. At Karakallou the tower
is the decisive feature of the whole building, which for the rest is
more or less modern, though in no way disagreeable.

While we were dining in an amusing circular Turkish room, we
hear the beating of a *symandron* in the courtyard. It was not yet the
hour for the evening service, and the rhythm which was being beaten
was not the usual unmistakable one. Instead, it turned out to be a
special rhythm for the cats. On hearing it, they came rushing into the
courtyard from all sides, from doors, windows and dark holes. In a
few minutes there were twenty or thirty round the monk with the
symandron, who led them to a recess in one corner of the court, set
aside as the cats' dining-room, where they were given their meal.

*It was founded *c.* A.D. 1000.

They were, of course, all of them tomcats, and they seemed very hungry. As it was a Wednesday, it was a fast-day (Karakallou is the only coenobian monastery on the east coast). And the cats as well as the monks received only one meal. Presumably, however, they didn't feel obliged to refrain from augmenting their diet in other ways.

The monastery of Philotheou is less than an hour's walk from Karakallou. After the country between Chilandari and Zographou, and the walks from St Anne's to Little St Anne's and from Kerassiá to Lavra, this tract is perhaps the finest part of Athos. It is extraordinarily rich and fertile with orchards, olives and trees of every kind, with numerous peasant-houses and hermitages.

Philotheou is surrounded by green meadows cut up by streams and brooks, like some English countryside. The monastery is irregular in shape and without any tower, not in any way striking, apart from its charming situation. Most of it was rebuilt after a fire in the last century. But the work has been done with good taste, following the style of the earlier buildings.

The venerable porter took a special interest in us. He told us his whole story, as we walked up and down on the lawn in front of the entrance porch. He was the ambitious younger son of a restaurant keeper in a small town in Messenia.

'My one idea was to make a great deal of money,' he told us, 'and when I was twenty, that is, in 1897, I emigrated to America. I landed in New York and managed to find a job as a cook, but it was badly paid, and after some months, as nothing better turned up, I decided to try my luck in Canada. In a small industrial town I found work in an ammunition factory. I got on fairly well there, and was soon earning quite a lot of money, compared at least to what I had been making previously in New York. But I wasn't at all satisfied. There were three other Greeks working in the same town, who kept speaking to me about Alaska, about the new mines which had been discovered there, and the vast possibilities there were for making a fortune. It was mid-winter, and they had made up their minds to go to Alaska as soon as the season was a little more advanced. I was very tempted to accompany them, and the only thing that kept me back was the fact that I was in love with a girl in the town I was working in, and I couldn't bear the idea of such a long separation from her. Virginia was half Greek and half American. We were on very intimate terms; she seemed to return my love, and had promised to marry me. My desire to make money was still terribly strong, and I don't know what I should have decided to do; but one night I went into a dancing place and saw Virginia with one of the three Greeks who wanted me to go with them to Alaska. He was called Jim. They were sitting in a separate niche, and he had his arm round her neck. Virginia pretended not to see me, and looked the other way, but she was obviously embarrassed. I called her away from the table; she was silent, and did not know what explanation to give. Then Jim came along to see what I wanted with her.

' "If you have anything to say, say it to me." he said.

'A scene followed in which we quarrelled wildly, but Virginia suddenly put a stop to it by saying:

' "What do you want from me? It's Jim I love.'

'The words shattered me, and I went away. I tried to forget Virginia, but from that moment I hated Jim and regarded him as an enemy.

'I decided to leave for Alaska and a few days later we started off, all four of us, Jim and I, and the two others. But the weather was bad, and at one point there had been a series of avalanches, so that the train didn't run all the way and we were obliged to walk a certain distance to a place where we could find another train. The railway line followed the edge of a long lake, which had been frozen for months, and we were advised that it would be far quicker for us to cut across the ice and join the line on the other side. So we sent out across the frozen lake.

'We had been walking for quite a time when suddenly I heard a cry behind me, and turning round saw that one of my companions had fallen through the ice above his waist. The ice, which he was holding on to, might give way if one went too close. Jim, who was the bravest of us, approached him, and threw him a rope, telling him to tie it round himself. But just as he got the rope fast, he began screaming in the most terrible way, shouting:

' "Help! Help! Something has bitten me."

'We tugged at the rope and drew him out of the water. But to our horror we saw the ice stained red with blood. Half the man's leg was gone. There was no help to be got. We were alone in the middle of the lake. We tied up his leg with some clothes and carried the poor fellow on our backs towards the coast. But on the way he died. We were afraid of dying from exposure too. As soon as we reached land we dug a hole and buried our companion under a little wooden cross and then walked on in silence.

'None of us spoke a word. The fate of our friend made us hard and wild inside. As we marched, we said to ourselves: "Either we go on and make a fortune, or we die by the road like him." We were now only three.

'At last we reached a train. The journey was long and slow. In two days we reached our destination. But the exposure and hardships we had gone through were too much for another of my companions. He got pneumonia, and died a few days later. Only Jim and I were left.

'We found work in the new gold-mines, and began to earn money. Jim kept receiving letters every now and then from Virginia. And each time he came and showed them to me. I said nothing, but my hatred of him grew all the time and completely filled my mind. I could have killed him. But in August, when the season's work was nearly over, an explosion took place where we were working in the mine. I and a few others ran and managed to escape; I was hit and wounded by falling blocks of stone, but not seriously. Jim, however, was very badly injured. We were brought to hospital and put in beds next to each other. A screen was put round Jim's bed to prevent the others seeing his terrible wounds. That night he called Virginia's name in his sleep. I began to pity him. Next day he managed to write her a letter, saying:

' "Perhaps I shall live, perhaps I shall die. But my last wish is, if I die, that you should try to forget me."

'He called the nurse and asked her to give me the letter. He said to me:

' "Either send it to her by post, or give it to her yourself: You are less ill, I think, than I am."

'His expression was so terribly pathetic that I felt very sorry for him, and ashamed of my hatred. So when the nurse went away I crept out of bed and asked his forgiveness for having wished him misfortune. Jim asked me to forgive him, too, if we had quarrelled.

'Next day he died.

'I felt I could not see Virginia again and posted the letter. Shortly afterwards I returned to Canada alone. In spite of my resolution I went to see Virginia. To my horror I found her mad: she didn't even recognise me. Her father said:

' "She has been like this since a letter arrived for her from Alaska."

'He didn't know the whole story of her love, and could understand nothing. I couldn't bear the sight of Virginia mad. I felt alone in the world, and somehow responsible for this series of catastrophes. Why had I been spared by God? What should I do now? I was filled with disgust by the thought of my past life, and its emptiness. I returned to Greece, to my home town in Messinia, hoping to be able to live there peacefully. But I could not rid myself of my melancholy, or find any rest for my soul. I had saved quite a respectable sum of money during my years in America, but what use was money to me when nothing one could do with it seemed anything but futile or idle? I went to a priest, and he advised me to become a monk. A year later I came to the Holy Mountain. I have been at Philotheou now for twenty years, and in renouncing all worldly ambition I have found the peace which was formerly denied me.'

17

Father Ambrose

I could not leave the Holy Mountain without going again to see Father Ambrose, whom I had met originally on my very first visit to Karyes. I had gone into the church of Protáton and after the dazzling sunlight only the rich iconostasis and the magnificent brass corona at first stood out. I thought I was alone, and was suddenly startled to hear a deep voice speaking from the ceiling, asking me if I were a 'European'. A monk was standing on a wooden platform, painting. He climbed down and explained that he was restoring some of the frescoes attributed to the semi-legendary Macedonian master Pansélinos. He was also making a copy of one of the heads for the Greek Governor of Athos.

On seeing I had a camera with me he asked whether I knew a lot about photography. He said he had a very good camera himself, but that his photographs were never successful.

'Photography is an art,' he said, 'and I have never studied it.'

He began asking all sorts of technical questions and suggested I should visit his house, which was quite close. He was called Father Ambrose and was an independent monk, attached to the Protáton, not to a monastery.

He collected his paints and brushes and locked the door of the church. We made some purchases in Karyes, turned up a small side-street, walked through some gardens and climbed a steep path among chestnut trees. In ten minutes we were at his house, a two-storied white building with greyish-blue windows and balconies. The main entrance was from the back, on to the first floor, owing to the slope of the ground. A very young monk opened the door and disappeared without a word. Two older monks also lived in the house, but both seemed to be there more or less in the capacity of servants.

The house inside had a curious charm. We went into the drawing-room. The walls were whitewashed. On one side was a fireplace and on the other a very long Turkish divan, running the whole length of the room. Over it were three good copies by Father Ambrose of Old

Masters: Salome, with the head of John the Baptist on a silver salver, St George as a youth in armour, and Christ with the thorn-wreath. A door and two windows gave on to a balcony, with a magnificent view over Karyes, its orchards, and the whole countryside down to the sea, with the islands of Lemnos and Thasos rising faintly in the the distance. In front was the rocky pyramid of Athos, shining in the sun.

We drank the traditional Turkish coffee, accompanied by the spoonful of delicious green jam, called *nerantza*, made from unripe oranges, and talked abut Lysippos and Alexander the Great. Father Ambrose told me that Lysippos had planned to carve the Mountain into a colossal statue of Alexander. In the one hand he was to have held a whole city, while water was to have fallen from the other in a great cascade. The entire army was to have been used for the work, but Alexander kept saying 'Later, later', as he was only interested in war and conquest, and died before anything could come of the project.

Afterwards Father Ambrose showed me over the whole house. There were seven rooms on the first floor, apart from the kitchen, which had running water, canalised from a spring in the mountain slope. None of the rooms were very large, but the ceilings were so low that they appeared bigger than they were. No fewer than three of them were studios, with numerous easels on which pictures were standing, mostly painted with enormous precision and care, almost like miniatures. One set of three large pictures of saints in gorgeous robes against a gold background had just been finished to the order of King Boris of Bulgaria, and were to decorate a church in Philippopolis. They were painted with astonishing technical ability in the traditional style of the Byzantine church.

Downstairs were storerooms, a carpenter's workshop, and a dark room for developing, ingeniously fitted up with a dark red windowpane. There was also a tiny chamber full of hens and chickens, who apparently spent their whole life imprisoned.

Whenever I passed through Karyes, I always made a point of visiting Father Ambrose. One day I helped him to photograph a large Madonna he had painted. He told me there were two kinds of Madonnas: 'the severe kind', with unnatural features which the Orthodox Church preferred, and the sweet-faced kind, which he called 'the cocotte Madonna'. His were of the latter – 'realistic' – variety.

Father Ambrose was intelligent, and one of the most refined types I had met on the Mountain, quite different from the ordinary monk, who is without any culture. Now, on my last stay in Karyes, when I went to say goodbye to him, I was anxious to hear more about his life.

He was sitting on the long divan in his drawing-room, and began to talk at once about his desire for a young man of some education who would be a companion to him. Father Ambrose was still strong and active, and though over sixty did not at all look his age. But this afternoon he spoke as an old man.

'The freshness of youth is passed; I need a young man who is sensitive, and understands something about art, to live with me these last years till I die. Could you help me to find someone? Anyone who came and lived with me would inherit a small fortune from me when I die.'

I promised to help him if I could, and began asking him about his past life.

'Ah, you want me to awaken old unhappy memories,' said Father Ambrose. 'I was born in Caesarea, in Cappadocia, and at the age of seventeen came to the Holy Mountain to become a monk. At first I lived at the skite of Kafsokalyvia under the peak of Athos, and there I learned to paint at the house of Father Josaphas, who was the best-known painter of sacred pictures. I remained there eighteen years.

'But as I am myself not a great painter, it was my dream to see real works of art, and the paintings of other countries. I had been told that there were wonderful pictures in Russia. I had saved a little money, and went off first to Athens. But the various pictures in the Gallery there did not please me very much. So I took a steamer to Odessa, and from there went by train to St Petersburg. It was a long journey, but it was there in fact I saw the most wonderful paint-ings; for nowhere else were there finer masterpieces than in Russia. Nowadays, it is perhaps different.

'I lived in St Petersburg in the house of a Greek lady. There was also a little boy of twelve living there, who did various odd jobs about the house. He was a lively, warm-hearted child, and showed interest and a good deal of talent for painting. Of course he had as yet no experience, and didn't paint well, but he gave the impression that he might one day do something good. He was particularly friendly to me, and ready to do anything I asked when I sent him with a message or to fetch colours, and so on; and he continually came to me and asked all sorts of questions about Mount Athos. At last I became curious about him and asked him who his mother was. "Oh, I don't know really, but I think the lady of the house is." But she didn't seem to be, for if she had been she would have sent the boy to school. I was so interested in him, however, that I asked her one day about his parents.

' "He is a poor unfortunate boy," she said. "I have had him here for five years."

' "And his mother?" I asked. "Is she no longer alive?"

' "No, she died five years ago, when she handed the child over to me. But if it interests you I'll tell you the whole story.

' "The child's parents were both Greek, and had three children, two very pretty daughters and this boy, who was much the youngest child. The father worked as a gardener for a very rich prince here in St Petersburg, but the family was so poor that it was always a terrible struggle to bring up the children.

' "One night the prince gave a great reception in his palace, to which the most elegant society of St Petersburg was invited; and, as extra servants were required for the occasion, the two daughters of the gardener, who were fifteen and seventeen years old, were engaged.

' "Next morning, neither of them came home. The father guessed what had happened and, quite mad with rage, ran to the prince to complain.

' " 'You are an impertinent fellow,' was the answer of the prince. 'If you choose to speak in that way again, I'll have you thrown out. If you were a good father, you would have kept your daughters always at home. Now, if you want them back, go and fetch them. One is sleeping with Count C., the other with Prince D., but I warn you: if you disturb these gentlemen at their pleasures you are a lost man. That you know.'

' "The father tried to speak, but was so shaken by this news that he broke down completely and began to weep.

' "The Prince simply said: 'It's no use making a fuss like this you had better go and see to the garden instead', and had him thrown out.

' "The gardener and his wife didn't know what to do, for they realised that if they went to the gentlemen in question and demanded their daughters back the father would lose his job, and then they would die of hunger, as they had no other possibilities of earning money. And so they remained with their little son, who was then six.

[112]

' "The distress of the father at losing his two daughters was so terrible that his hair turned white, and he became like an old man. A few months later he died.

' "His wife and child were sent away from the palace, as another gardener's family was engaged. The poor widow made every effort to see one of her daughters, and at last succeeded in arranging a short meeting. They embraced each other and kissed. The daughter gave her mother some money, but each of her words only served to show the enormous gulf that lay between them. The mother became more and more horrified at her daughters' life (they were both in the same brothel now), and at their apparent satisfaction with it.

' "She went away and tried to find work, but she was delicate, and what she found was far too rough and heavy for her to bear for long. She went to various houses hoping to find something better, and finally she came to me. I did what I could for her, Father Ambrose, but she had suffered too much and died shortly afterwards. Before that, however, she told me this story and said:

' " 'I leave you my child; please see that he never learns anything about his parents, or who his sisters are, help him to become a good man, and to follow the way of God.' " '

Father Ambrose paused.

'I was filled with such pity for the boy on hearing this story,' he went on, 'that I asked the lady what she would say to my taking him back with me to the Holy Mountain, and teaching him there to become a good painter, at the same time fulfilling his mother's wish.

' "It will be hard," she said, "I don't know if the boy, free as he is, will wish to lead a life so strict as that on Athos, unless we try to convince him that it is a wonderful country."

'I at once began to suggest to the boy that he should accompany me back to Athos. He was so happy to be with me that my idea delighted him. He wanted absolutely to accompany me. He regarded me as a relation, and each day we became closer friends.

'I remained another six or seven months in St Petersburg, and soon felt more than fatherly love for the boy. I don't know really what the feelings were that I had for him, but I wanted to do everything in my power to help him. He was so affectionate, too, and kissed me tenderly each morning.

'But one day he was no longer there. We searched everywhere for him, and informed the police. After a few days we discovered that a certain gentleman had him in his house. I immediately went to visit the gentleman in question and spent a long time trying to persuade him to give the boy back.

' "You must let him go," I said, "it is something sacred that he should go to the Holy Mountain."

'At last he agreed and fetched the boy, who didn't seem at all so pleased to leave. I was astonished: something in him seemed altered.

' "Do you want to come?" I asked.

' "Yes," he said, but without much conviction.

'I brought him home, and two days later we left for Mount Athos.

'While in St Petersburg I had sold a number of pictures I had been commissioned to paint, so that I had saved a fair sum of money. I bought this house and furnished it as well as I could, and here we lived together.

'The boy could not adapt himself very easily to a monk's life, but after a time he seemed to get used to it and I was happy.

'The months slipped by. He was now fourteen, and showed even keener interest in drawing and painting. He had done some pencil drawings so astonishing that I was convinced he would one day become a great painter. And I was so fond of him.

'One evening after dinner, when he came to me as usual to kiss me before going to bed, he said: "I shall stay with you tonight; we will sleep together," he said, "I feel the need to be with someone."

'He undressed and got into my bed.

'From that night I became his plaything.

'That lasted two years; I thought I was in an earthly paradise, but when he was sixteen or so, he began often to be depressed and dissatisfied. At such times he drew faces with wicked expressions which were quite extraordinary. And in the rare moments when he was happy, he drew angels with smiling faces which were a marvel of beauty.

'From time to time I received letters from the lady in St Petersburg, asking me how the boy was, and if he were happy. But it was painful for me to write about the boy, and after what had happened between us, I would rather not have written at all.

'Then one day a yacht came here. It belonged to a young American, who came and visited me and saw the drawings of the boy, who always wrote his name and age on them. The American was so impressed that he wanted to meet him. Something in me told me not to let them see each other; but the American gave me no peace and begged again and again. At last I called the boy. The meeting was quite short, but the American came back several times between visits to various monasteries, and finally asked me to let him show the boy the yacht.

'When the boy came back in the evening, he was completely changed.

'In an expressionless voice, he said: "You know, I am going away."

'I had rather a thunderbolt had destroyed the whole house than hear those words.

'I tried to persuade him not to go away; I begged him for my sake to remain. He didn't listen. I think that I even wept. But it was useless. Nothing availed to alter his decision. At last I saw that noting could be done, and said:

' "Very well, if you want to go, I shall not prevent you. The only thing I ask you to do for me is to promise to write me how you are getting on, and where you are."

'That night for the first time for two years he slept alone.

'I could not sleep at all. The American visited me the next morning and explained that he wanted the boy to have the chance to study properly.

' "Why should he always have to remain on Mount Athos, without any opportunities to develop his art, without prospects in life?" he said.

' "I see," I muttered, with my heart as heavy as stone, and went into my room. A few minutes later the boy came in, quite shy and awkward, as if he were really sorry for what he was doing. He took my hand and wanted to kiss me, but I wouldn't let him. Then he began to cry.

' "It would have been better if you had gone away without saying goodbye," I said.

' "But you forget that I am young," he replied, "that I must live. I want to live! I want my freedom! And you know I shall never forget you: I shall always love you, even when I am far away."

'He put his arms round me, and kissed me. Then I heard the door of the house shut. I fell on the bed. I was alone.'

Father Ambrose stared in front of him without saying another word. I saw the pain in his expression. He buried his face in his hands.

After some time he said:

'I heard from him from Athens, then from Constantinople, then from Italy. In each letter he wrote that he was happier than ever. He wrote three other times from America; in the last letter he said he had had great successes and had become a teacher in an academy of art. Let it be so. I hope he won't write again. You see what I meant when I said that the freshness of youth is gone. Youth demands youth.'

Father Ambrose was silent. A soft wind from the sea came through the window. The peak of Athos was violet in the last rays of the sun. I rose and left the painter, who scarcely noticed my departure.

Our weeks on Mount Athos had come to an end. Two days later we were back in Salonica.

Monk at Grand Lavra

The monastery of Gregoriou on the steep and rocky west coast

The coenobian monastery of St Paul's

Looking over the roofs of Stavronikita towards Mount Athos

The brigands: photograph in Father Savvas's cell at Grigoriou

Monk and Iorgos in the court of Grand Lavra

One of the hermits at Karoulia

Russian monk fishing for his supper

Monk investigating the camera

Monk telling a story

The hermit settlement of Karoulia

Young painter-monk at Kafsokalyvia

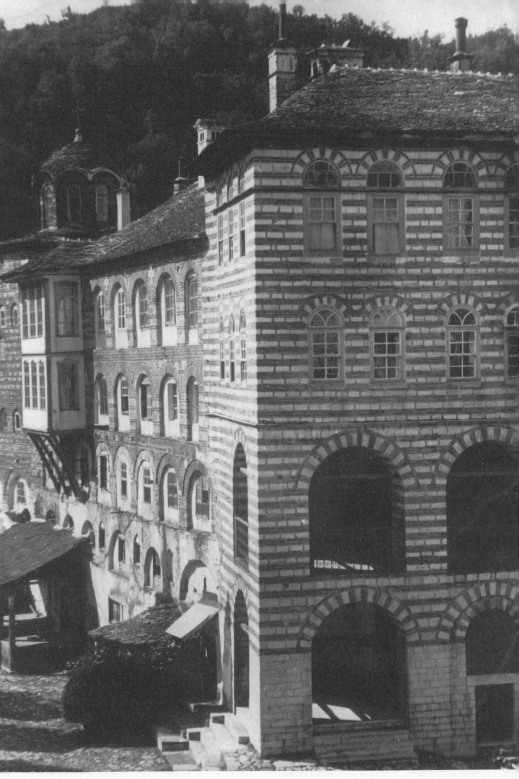

The guest house at the Serbian monastery of Chilandari

The monastery of Karakallou

Students at the Hierarchical College at Karyes

Young novice at Karyes

Appendices

APPENDIX I

MONASTERIES	FOOD	ROOMS	BUGS*	W.C
Koutloumoussiou	very bad	primitive	millions	disgusting
Iviron	good	good	none	questionable
Xiropotamou	not bad	decent	none	very dirty
Pantokrator	just eatable	simple, but marvellous view	none	linger in for view
Stavronikita	good	?	?	?
Vatopèdi	good; dull	very good	none	real water-closet
Esphigmenou	good; varied	good	none	worth visiting for sake of architecture
Chilandari	Serbian cooking; best on Athos	good	none	decent
Zographou	practically uneatable	horrid	quantities	passable
Kastamonitou	trouble taken, unsuccessful	Turkish, picturesque	none	?
Dochiariou	disgusting, worst on Athos	best on Athos	not one	decent
Xenophontos	just eatable	decent	some	average
St Pantaleïmon	Salty; interesting	very respectable	none	unattractive
Gregoriou	excellent	respectable	none	very clean
Simópetra	not too bad	bourgeois	no	striking
Dionysiou	unappetising, below average	depressing, light	no	horrible
St Paul's	dull	without charm	sometimes	?
Lavra	disgraceful	Turkish gloom	yes	unmentionable
Karakallou	not too bad	simple, clean, marvellous view	no	passable
Philotheou	just eatable	uninteresting	no	passable
St Anne's	not at all bad	primitive	a fair amount	?
Kerassiá	Russian, very good	pleasant	no	?
Kafsokalyvia	very good	very nice	no	uninviting, woods at hand
Karyes	well cooked	simple	no	uncomfortable

*I cannot guarantee that this list is completely accurate – as I took special precautions against attacks, and as the height of the season was past.

History

Mount Athos is frequently mentioned in ancient literature. Even in mythology it plays its part. On its summit was one of the chain of fires that brought to Mycenae the news that Troy had fallen; there still can be seen traces of the canal cut across the isthmus by Xerxes to avoid the danger of having his fleet wrecked in passing round its stormy promontory. Later there were flourishing cities on the slopes of the Mountain. The legends, too, which relate to the first years of the Christian era are very numerous. The Virgin herself and St John are supposed to have been the first to convert it, when they were driven there by a storm on their way to Cyprus. But virtually nothing is known about Athos during these early centuries. The ancient cities must have died out, and hermits may have come to live among the rocks.

The first historical records of their residence date from the ninth century. It is very possible that they chose Athos as a refuge from the violence of the iconoclastic controversy. Peter the Athonite and Euthemius of Salonica are the first we know by name. These early monks lived in caves. Towards the end of the century, however, a more organised type of settlement arose, though still looser than that of a real monastery. An imperial charter of 875 established the monastery of Kolobos at Ierisos, just north of Xerxes's canal, as protector of the monks of Athos, and at the same time admitted the rights of the monks as owners of the Mountain. When, shortly after-wards, the monastery began to abuse its rights, the monks sent a deputy to appeal to the Emperor Leo VI. They won their case, and their representative, Andreas, was created head of the community, with the title of Protos, an office which continued till the seventeenth century. Karyes was already the centre of the community, and the church of Protáton was built about A.D. 950.

The first real monastery on Mount Athos was founded in 963 by St Athanasius, the friend and confessor of the Emperor Nicephorus Phocas, who helped with gifts of money and declared the monastery free from all authority – except that of the Emperor. After Phocas was murdered his successor John Tzimiskes continued the imperial support by further grants of money. St Athanasius died in A.D. 1000.

Already during his lifetime a number of other monasteries were founded, and the movement continued to gather strength after his death. But at the same time the numbers of hermits under the Protos continued to grow. A conflict was inevitable, and finally the Emperor Constantine IX drew up a charter in 1046, in part reiterating the previous constitution, but further declaring that the General Assembly was to be composed mainly of the abbots of the monasteries. The Protos, representative of the hermits, was reduced to quite a subordinate position, and the hermitages gradually passed into the control of the monasteries, whose greater efficiency and co-ordination had in any case made their final success inevitable. In 1094 Alexius Comnenus declared the Mountain independent of the bishops of Ierisos and Salonica.

The development of the rest of the world in the succeeding centuries had very little influence on the inner life on Athos. It has had periods of brilliance: at the beginning of the thirteenth century 300 monasteries are mentioned as existing. And it has lived through periods of disastrous depopulation and savage attacks from outside enemies, especially during the time of the Latin Empire, when Pope Innocent III himself had to interfere to protect the monks, and at the beginning of the fourteenth century, owing to the atrocities of an army of Catalan mercenaries. More stable conditions returned, however, and by the end of the century nineteen of the twenty monasteries existing at the present day had already been established. From this period on, the principal conflicts that the Mountain had to undergo were internal.

In the first half of the sixteenth century there arose on Athos an extraordinary theological controversy which shook the whole Orthodox world. A certain monk discovered one day that after a long period of fasting and profound meditation on his navel, he could see the Divine Light of Mount Tabor. His example was quickly followed by many other monks who also saw the Divine Light. A manuscript by Abbot Xerocarca still exists, describing the spiritual exercises required as a preliminary to seeing the Uncreated Light.

Sit down in a corner [he writes], shut your door and raise your spirit above everything vain and temporary; then bend your beard forward on your breast, and with all your soul open the perceiving eye which is in the middle of our body. Restrict the exits of the air so that you should not breathe too easily. Force yourself to find the exact site of the heart, where all the forces of your soul are destined to live. First you will encounter darkness, and the resistance of impenetrable masses; but if you persevere and continue with this work day and night, you will finish by feeling an inexprimable joy; because as soon as you have found the site of the heart, the spirit sees that which it could never realise previously. It then sees the air between it and the heart glowing, clearly and perceptibly, with a miraculous light.*

It is difficult, perhaps, at first sight, to see why this discovery of some hermits should have such significance. But the deduction was drawn that the light which could be seen in such a way was uncreated. Opponents to such a theory arose at once, declaring that God alone was uncreated. A Calabrian monk, Barlaam, wrote a pamphlet against the 'navel-souled ones'. But the mystics, too had their supporters, and the dispute spread. Even the Emperor and the Patriarch were involved, and the matter was fought out through a series of Councils. Finally, a Council at Constantinople decided the matter in favour of the mystics, declaring that the light which they saw was really the Divine Light of Mount Tabor. The party of Barlaam was anathematised as heretic, and peace returned to the Holy Mountain.

In the fifteenth century a new and important change took place in the organisation of the Athonic monasteries. Until this time all the monasteries were coenobian. Government was under an abbot. All property was held in common, even clothes being shared. Meals were taken in common and attendance at services, etc., was compulsory. But with the growth of wealth came the demand for a freer and more individual system, resulting in the adoption by many monasteries of idiorhythmy. In an idiorhythmic monastery government is by a committee. The monks have their meals individually in their cells and within reasonable limits are free to attend services or not. They are even allowed to possess money.

An idiorhythmic monastery is naturally more expensive to run than a coenobian, and at time of impoverishment and decay a return to the stricter rule was usually one of the first steps taken. On such

*From an article by R. Fülop-Miller in *La Nazione* (Florence) April, 1935.

occasions a hermit of pious reputation used often to be called in, like the philosopher in ancient Greece, to decide on the necessary steps. Some monasteries have changed their rule a number of times, and at the present day eleven are coenobian, and nine, in the main the richer ones, are idiorhythmic, being managed in a more commercial and less spiritual manner.

External affairs left the Mountain unchanged. Even the submission to the Turks in 1430, after the fall of Salonica, had little effect. The monks were cut off from the Emperor, but they preserved their autonomy, and secured in a way a greater degree of independence than ever before. There were raids from pirates and taxation was high. But new benefactors took the place of the old, especially the Princes of Moldo-Wallachia; and monks were sent on begging tours through the whole Orthodox world.

During the Greek Revolution the Holy Mountain had to pay a large indemnity to the Turks for their support of Greece, and in return the new Greek State confiscated a considerable portion of the monastic estates in 1834, on the grounds that a 'medieval system was incompatible with a modern State'. The century saw other serious financial losses: in 1862 the Rumanian government sequestrated the vast properties owned there by the monks, the donations of centuries, producing an income of £120,000 annually. Athos, declaring that the act was illegal, refused to accept an indemnity. The final disaster was the Russian Revolution, which left the Russians on Athos altogether deprived of outside support.

The period of Turkish sovereignty ended in 1912. A period of uncertainty as to who should control the Mountain followed, but in 1923 Greece was granted the sovereignty over the monks by the Treaty of Lausanne, and in 1927 the Constitution of Athos was ratified by the Government.

Organisation and Administration

The twenty sovereign monasteries of Mount Athos are autonomous, and control their own affairs of all kinds. And it is to them that the whole land of Athos belongs.

As has already been explained however, there exist two forms of monasteries – the coenobian and the idiorhythmic. At the present time eleven monasteries follow the older, coenobian rules. The head of the monastery is the abbot, who must be a person of general education. But it is only in spiritual matters that he is absolute. In administrative and financial matters he must act in consultation with two or three epitropes, who are elected annually by the elders (Ierondas) out of their own number. Certain questions require the consent of the whole body of elders, while the whole assembly of monks is alone capable of deciding changes in general policy.

Idiorhythmic monasteries are not under an abbot, but are administered by the epitropes, who are the executive officials. They are annually elected by the 'superiors' (*proestamenoi*) out of their own number. The 'superiors' comprise about ten per cent of the monastery, and have the right to co-opt new members. They alone have a say in administration, and the government is thus oligarchical. The administrative class receives salaries for its work.

Fully half the monks on the Holy Mountain do not live in the monasteries. There is a large variety of other forms of life. Of these the most important are the skites. Each is dependent on the monastery on whose land it is built. A skite may be idiorhythmic or coenobian, without relation to the rule followed by the parent house. Each kind of skite, however, lives under a prior, the *dikaios*, and the main administrative difference is merely that the idiorhythmic prior is elected for one year, not for life.

Today there are twelve skites scattered about the Mountain. The majority consist of separate small houses near a central church, and without any surrounding wall. They are, indeed, like villages. Two or three, however, the 'Serail', for example, are great blocks like monasteries, and in some cases they are larger than their parent houses. The monastery controls the election of officials. It also rents the houses of the skite directly to the inmates.

A still smaller unit is the *kellion*, a little cottage usually with a plot of ground attached, rented by three or at the most six monks directly from the monastery to whom the ground belongs. Over 200 *kellia* exist on the Mountain.

Further there are *kalyvae*, small isolated cottages for one or two monks, *athismata*, still smaller dwellings, and *hesychasteria*, retreats mostly in precipitous out-of-the-way parts. In the case of the two latter types, the monastery has the obligation of providing the inmates with bread.

The Holy Mountain is governed by two bodies: the Holy Community (Koinotis), and the Epistasia, whose members reside permanently in Karyes. The Holy Community consists of twenty members, elected annually, one from each monastery, and meets three times a week. It is the legislative body and has the duties of preserving tradition, of settling disputes between monasteries, acting as the Court of Appeal, and of preserving the peace, etc. Communications of general interest made to the Greek Government or to the Patriarch are its concern.

The Epistasia is the executive body. It consists of four members, each of whom keeps one part of the official seal of Athos. The twenty monasteries are divided into four groups of five, one of which takes control of the Epistasia each year. The head of the Epistasia is at the same time the president of the Holy Community.

In carrying out its work, the Epistasia has at its command a local guard. If necessary, however, it may call in the State police to assist it.

APPENDIX IV

Calendar, Services, Fasting

Athos still keeps to the old calendar, and this seemingly innocent topic is actually one of the most violently and widely discussed. The monks claim that the Government wishes to expel them for not adopting the modern calendar, and the one monastery that has done so, Vatopèdi, the richest and most elegant, is universally despised for its spirit of innovation. Other monasteries refuse to send representatives to its feasts.

But in addition to preserving the old calendar, Mount Athos has a system of time peculiar to itself. Byzantine time is adopted: that is, 12 o'clock is not at midday, but at sunset, and thus is not a fixed point, but varies with the season. Clocks must be changed every few days. Again, Vatopèdi is the sole exception to the rule.

At sunset the gates of all the monasteries are locked and barred for the night. They must not be reopened until dawn.

A large proportion of the day and night are taken up by services. Monasteries of course vary among themselves in the amount of time given to services: in the idiorhythmic monasteries there is a tendency to get through with them as quickly as possible, while in some of the severer coenobian monasteries they are drawn out to twice the normal length.

Fasting plays an enormous rôle on Mount Athos. To begin with, there are certain foods that it is impossible to get. As there are no female animals, milk and butter are unobtainable, except in tins at Karyes. Cheese is a comparative rarity. Since a fairly recent decision of the Holy Koinotis hens are allowed to be kept by idiorhythmic monasteries outside their walls, but it is still difficult to find eggs when one wants them.

Apart from such natural difficulties, fasting is particularly strictly observed. In 'coenobia', meat is forbidden at any time, and if something containing meat is ordered for a monk by the doctor, it must be prepared outside the walls. Idiorhythmic monks can eat meat in their cells, but it must not be prepared in the main kitchen of the monastery. Further, in coenobian monasteries Mondays, Wednesdays and Fridays are regular fasting days. Only one meal is eaten, at midday, and the permitted foods are limited by the exclusion of all oils and fats. Even idiorhythmic houses restrict to a certain extent their diet on Wednesdays and Fridays, without, however, reducing the number of meals. Finally, there are the great fasts preceding Christmas, Easter, the feast of the Apostles Peter and Paul, and the Assumption, varying from two to seven weeks.

Population

Monasteries	No. of monks	District from which monks are principally recruited
Koutloumoussiou (coen.)	39	Leukas and Xante islands
Iviron (id.)	117	Mainly from the Diocese of Myriophyto (Macedonia)
Stavronikita (id.)	18	Greeks outside Greece
Pantokrator (id.)	40	Salonica and Hellespont
Vatopèdi (id.)	97	Turkey (mainly Constantinople district) and Chalcidice
Esphigmenou (coen.)	45	Peloponnesos
Chilandari (id.)	57	Serbians and Bulgarians
Zographou (coen.)	77	Bulgarians (especially Macedonian
Kastamonitou (coen.)	42	Asia Minor and islands
Dochiariou (id.)	44	Constantinople
Xenophontos (coen.)	52	Lesbos and mainland opposite
St Pantaleïmon (coen.)	375	Russia
Xiropotamou (id.)	61	Turkey
Simópetra (coen.)	43	Erythrean Peninsula
Gregoriou	53	Peloponnesos
Dionysiou (coen.)	54	Exclusively Greeks from Turkey
St Paul's (coen.)	52	Cephalonia
Lavra (id.)	116	Greek (mixed) – master and pupil must be of the same nationality.
Karakallou (coen.)	53	Epirus
Philotheou (id.)	43	Greeks outside Greece

Principal Skites	Dependent on	No. of monks
St Andrew (Serail)	Vatopèdi	c. 100 (Little Russians)
Prophet Elias	Pantokrator	c. 100 (Russians)

Robert, I tried to have
this in time for your
birthday — but it was on
back order. Anyway, Happy
Birthday.

Edward

P.S. Come over sometime & tell
us about your trip to England.

MOONRISE, HERNANDEZ, NEW MEXICO c. 1941

Photograph by ANSEL ADAMS

PUBLISHED BY MUSEUM GRAPHICS • P.O. BOX 5157, REDWOOD CITY, CALIFORNIA 94063 • FULTONES™ BY GARDNER FULMER LITHOGRAPH

A-002-95

Nea Skite	St Paul's	*c.* 100
St Anne's	Lavra	*c.* 150
Kafsokalyvia	Lavra	*c.* 100
Prodrom (St John the Baptist)	Lavra	54
		(Rumanians, mostly Wallachians)
St Pantaleïmon	Koutloumoussïou	*c.* 43
Annunciation	Xenophontos	*c.* 50
St Demetrius of Salonica Vatopèdi		*c.* 42
Karyes (1928 census)		305

A very large number of monks live in smaller settlements and *kellia*.

The Greek census of 1928 gave for Mount Athos a total population of monks of 4,858. It can thus be seen that more than half the monks live outside the monasteries.

In addition there is a floating population of roughly 2,000 peasants (men and boys), a few of whom live permanently on the Mountain, while others have their families abroad. Most of them come from the islands and the mainland nearby, as well as the part of Macedonia bordering on Albania.

Architecture on Mount Athos

The conditions of danger and uncertainty prevailing in the Eastern Mediterranean had their natural effect on the architectural plan of the Athonic monasteries. Even in the early nineteenth century there was always the possibility of an attack by pirates. Except, therefore, for those built in quite modern times, all the monasteries are fortified. The typical plan is for the buildings to form a more or less regular square, surrounded on the outside by strong walls, and with the windows facing the court in the centre. During the last century, however, two or more stories have often been added (as at Iviron) with windows and balconies above the walls looking out over the fields. Normally, there is only one gateway fitted with a series of floors. A tower is almost always to be found at some point in the enclosing walls: it was designed as a refuge in times of need, and nowadays has generally been converted into a library.

The church, except in one or two cases, stands free in the court along with the refectory and sacred well.

In the case of those monasteries which have harbours, there is generally an arsenal tower, into the bottom storey of which boats could be drawn on the approach of pirates.

The Athonic monastery is an independent organism, complete with buildings for servants, and, where necessary, an olive-mill and wine-press.

Owing to hostile raids and innumerable fires, by far the greater part of the buildings on Mount Athos are of comparatively recent age – since 1700 – but owing to the conservatism of the Mountain they have often been rebuilt in the older style. The churches, because they stand free in the court, have usually suffered less, and architecturally they are the most important feature.

CHURCHES

In Byzantine architecture there are two very distinct periods of bloom. The first of these, and by far the greatest, covers the fifth and sixth centuries, and those churches from that period which still remain are perhaps the finest in the world.

The really characteristic element in Byzantine churches is the cupola, a feature hitherto unknown in architecture. The cupola was invented in the third and fourth centuries in Armenia, and reached its highest expression in St Sophia's in Constantinople (523-7), where one can fully realise the revolutionary importance of its discovery. The architect of St Sophia achieved the extraordinary feat of raising a dome of 100 ft. diameter on pendentives over a square. From that moment domes were constructed everywhere, but the record of St Sophia has never been beaten.* Even the dome of St Peter's in Rome, which is raised on an octagon, a much easier accomplishment, has a diameter of only 80 ft.

During this first and greatest period of Byzantine architecture, churches were built on five distinct plans:

1st type: The old Hellenistic basilica, without a cupola, continues to be built.

Examples: St Paraskevi, Salonica, *c.* 450
St Demetrius, Salonica, *c.* 550
St Apollinare in Classe, Ravenna, *c.* 536-550
St Apollinare Nuovo, Ravenna, *c.* 526

2nd type: Cupola on a circular or polygonal base, surrounded at the most by an aisle, with occasionally a gallery above. In idea these churches derive fundamentally from the Pantheon.

Examples: St Costanza, Rome ⎱ both round, date from
St George, Salon ⎰ the fourth century
SS Sergius and Bacchus, ⎱ both
Constantinople, *c.* 520 ⎰ octagonal
St Vitale, Ravenna, 526-44

3rd type: Cupola raised on pendentives over the square formed by the intersection of the arms of a Greek cross. These churches have, from the outside, the shape of a square.

Earliest example: St Sophia, Salonica, *c.* 500. Also Kalendre Hané, Constantinople, *c.* 600.

*The Selim mosque at Adrianople has an equally large cupola, but raised on an octagon – a simpler accomplishment.

4th type: Greek cross plan standing quite free, with five cupolas, one on each of the arms of the cross, and the fifth at the intersection. This type is a development of the preceding one.

Original example: Holy Apostles, Constantinople (536-46), destroyed in fifteenth century.

Later examples following the plan of this church:
St Mark's, Venice, 1043-73
St Front, Périgueux, after 1120
Selim Mosque, Ephesus, 1375

5th type: Cupola over a square, with, in addition, apses equal in diameter to the cupola at each end, and surrounded by an aisle with a gallery above.

Example: St Sophia, Constantinople, 532-37 (cupola rebuilt 562). It forms a class for itself, and was not copied until after the fall of the Eastern Empire, when the Turks adopted it as a model for several of their mosques.

St Sophia in Salonica (3rd type), built abut A.D. 500, is important as being the prototype of the later Byzantine church, which became standardised, and continues to be built in Greece in the present day. In St Sophia, Salonica, however, the features of the later churches are many of them present only to a limited degree. The whole building has something rather experimental about it. The dome is only 33 ft. wide, a third of the diameter of St Sophia in Constantinople, and yet it is the largest in Greece. Indeed, after the reign of Justinian (527-65), Byzantine churches became smaller and smaller, until about the year A.D. 1000 they had reached quite Lilliputian dimensions. And by this time the features of the new style, based on the Greek cross in the square, had made themselves clear.

All these later churches are domed, and on the outside square or nearly so. The development of the Greek cross as the typical form was very natural. The cupola was supported by four piers joined by arches and these arches lengthened as barrel-vaults to form an abutment for the dome on its pendentives. Four small squares were thus left at the corners of the big square, and these, too, were usually covered by small cupolas.

But the chief characteristic of these churches, apart from their extreme smallness, is that the domes are raised on drums. Their diameter is often so small, and the drum so high in proportion, that from a distance the church gives the appearance of having turrets instead of cupolas. This raising of the cupola on a drum may add sometimes to the picturesqueness of the exterior of the church, but it is a considerable loss to the interior. The dome, especially when covered with mosaics, gives the interior of a church an atmosphere of mysticism. This feeling can be realised at its best perhaps in St Sophia in Constantinople, but also to a lesser degree in St Mark's, Venice, and St Sophia, Salonica, as well as in certain mosques. If, however, the great semi-spherical surface of the dome, which creates this mystical atmosphere, is raised on a drum, it loses its effect and the higher the drum the more evident is the loss.

St Sophia, Salonica has a drum, but it is so low that the impact of the cupola does not suffer. In the later churches, however, when the height of the drum is often more than the width of the dome, one has no feeling of having a dome above one, but only of a long tube riding from the roof. Practically all Renaissance and Baroque churches have cupolas raised on drums, and for that reason their interior is usually a failure. The few exceptions, such as the sacristy of San Lorenzo and the Capella dei Pazzi in Florence, are only on a relatively small scale.

In Constantinople the most important churches of this later type are:

The Gul Djami, or Rose Mosque (St Theodosia), ninth century

St Mary Pam, tenth century

St Theodore Tyrone, eleventh century

Saviour Pantepoptes, 1081 to 1118

Pantokrator *c.* 1124-26

In Salonica the principal churches of this type are the churches of St Elias* and of the Holy Apostles, the latter being the best of its kind in Greece. Both are twelfth century.†

In these churches, starting with St Theodore, Constantinople, one can observe a new departure in decoration. During the earlier Byzantine period, in the fifth and sixth centuries, one sees a certain inattention to exterior effect. In the tenth, eleventh and twelfth centuries, however, the outside is even more carefully designed than the inside. The earlier churches were built of brick, usually plastered over. In St

* Inscription says 1054: not a proof.
† Diehl suggests 1312 to 1315 but without authority. Both churches are probably twelfth century.

Theodore brick is still the material, but it is left bare and used in conjunction with bands of stone.

In these later churches blank walls between doors and windows are filled up with niches or wide flutings. All sorts of decorative effects are secured by setting bricks edgeways, forming zigzags, trellis-work and diamonds. The Church of the Holy Apostles in Salonica is the most inventive and the most successful example of this form of decorative work.

The innumerable churches on Mount Athos all follow more or less this later plan, but with certain distinguishing additions. They have the form of a Greek cross in a square, with a cupola at the intersection of the arms of the cross, an apsidal chancel flanked by side-chapels and cupolas raised on drums. So far they are normal. But the churches on Mount Athos have the rare feature of having apsidal ends to the transepts. The church of Lavra was the prototype, and all the other churches on the Mountain adopted the idea. In origin it may have been taken from Armenia (St Athanasius, the founder of Lavra, was from Trebizond). The few other cases where such transepts are found (St Elias in Salonica, and some thirteenth- and four-teenth-century Serbian churches) are definitely later.

From the outside the Athonic churches have rather the shape of a Latin cross, owing to the addition at the west end of a kind of anti-church, often, as at Dochiariou, larger than the church itself. The anti-church, or narthex, consists generally of six vaults supported by two columns, and is flanked by chapels. Very frequently the narthex is divided into two parts called *lite* and *mesonyktikon*. The origin of this large anti-church was presumably the smallness of the church proper, which was not big enough to contain all the monks of the monastery. Most Athonic churches have, in addition, an exterior loggia or exo-narthex, often glazed and giving the appearance of a conservatory. The narthex is normally contemporaneous with the church itself, while the exo-narthex has usually been built on later.

The outsides of the churches on Mount Athos are nearly always ruined by their being painted bright red. The practice dates in all probability from the earliest period, as the churches are almost all built of rubble and plastered over. Fortunately, there are a few exceptions to the rule. The churches at Chilandari, Dochiariou, Xiropotamou, St Anne's, one of the chapels at Lavra, and a few other small chapels have brick and stone exteriors. They all, however, Chilandari and Dochiariou excepted, date from the eighteenth century. The church at Chilandari (1290) is as it stands the oldest and externally the finest on Athos. The walls are decorated in polychrome with elaborate tile work accentuating the architectural lines. There are many doors on the sides, a Serbian feature.

The churches on Mount Athos are almost invariably disappointing inside, because, besides having the domes raised on high drums, every inch of wall space is painted over with dark frescoes which create a gloomy effect. Frescoes are a poor substitute for the mosaic decoration of the earlier Byzantine churches. Mosaics are, to begin with, far more suited to the covering of curved surfaces, and, further, are capable of glowing even in a dark room, where frescoes are scarcely visible. The only mosaics on Mount Athos are three panels surrounding the door leading into the narthex of the Vatopèdi church. Perhaps the best interior is that of the sixteenth-century church of Dionysiou. The cupola is on a somewhat shorter drum than usual, pentagonal on the outside. The frescoes are good, though in common with all paintings on the Holy Mountain they have been restored at a later date.

Properly speaking, there is very little Byzantine work on Athos. The only churches built prior to 1453 (the fall of the Byzantine Empire) are the following: the churches of the Protàton at Karyes (c. 950, very primitive and without a cupola though with good proportions), of Iviron, Lavra, Vatopèdi, Chilandari, and Pantokrator. And all of these, except Chilandari, have been remodelled at later times.

The main periods of building on Mount Athos are from 1500 to 1550, and from 1750 till the Greek Revolution. The church at Dochiariou (1568) shows certain new features derived from Moldo-Wallachia. It is unique in having buttresses. The roof plan in simplified, and the body of the church and the drums of the cupolas are abnormally high. The effect is a little ridiculous from the inside, but quite attractive from the exterior. These latter features had a certain influence on later structures.

During the second period of building, in the eighteenth century, there was a revival of a purer Byzantine style. Bricks and stone were used attractively in bands, though never with the elaboration and refinement found in the tenth to thirteenth centuries. The best example of a church in this style is perhaps that at Xiropotamou.

Enormous care has been lavished on decorating the interior of the churches, quite apart from the covering of every available square foot with frescoes, to which all architectural features have been sacrificed.

The floor is usually a mosaic of marble laid in geometrical patterns. The whole space of the church, however, is filled with ornaments, which create rather a cramped atmosphere. There are Syrian tables of ivory and mother-of-pearl for relics, reading desks, and innumerable sacred icons, covered with plates of beaten metal. The columns supporting the dome are often so hidden that only the capitals remain visible.

One of the most important features of the churches is the iconostasis, or screen, dividing the chancel from the body of the nave. Most of the screens on Mount Athos are of walnut wood, carved in high relief and gilded. They form a magnificent frame for a double row of sacred pictures, and do much to give life and dignity to the dark gloom of the church. The best examples, dating from the seventeenth century but following late Renaissance patterns, are in the churches of the Protáton, of Pantokrator and of Iviron. In the latter one can see traces of the earlier marble screen behind. In the nineteenth century there was a return to the marble screen. But all these new iconostases are crude work.†

Every church has, too, a 'corona', an elaborate circular brass candelabra, which hangs by chains from the cupola. It is made of twelve sections of brass plate, each rising in an arch in the centre, leaving room for a sacred picture (one of the apostles) with a pyramid of candles above, and joined together by double eagles. Vatopèdi and the church of the Protáton have particularly fine examples. In practically every case they are very decorative; even the early nineteenth-century church of St Pantaleïmon has one full of charm, with a silvery colour. Their only drawback is that they do much to block the view.

REFECTORIES

The refectory in those monasteries where there is sufficient space usually stands facing the main door of the church. It often has an open gallery running along the front. The best and oldest examples are T-shaped, though some are in the form of a Greek cross,‡ or even

*The finest floors on Athos are at Chilandari (1197) and Iviron; many are quite modern.
† Lavra, St Paul's, Kastamonitou, Xenophontos.
‡ Xiropotamou, St Pantaleïmon (nineteenth century).

a simple rectangle. Lavra has perhaps the finest (1512), though the refectories at Dochiariou (1547), Xenophontos and Dionysiou (both sixteenth century) are also very attractive and well-proportioned.

PHIALE

The *phiale*, or sacred well, usually stands between the church and the refectory. It consists of a cupola resting on eight or more columns. Lavra has the finest example: a porphyry basin surrounded by eight columns with Turkish stalactite capitals and connected by tenth-century marble slabs. The cupola, however, gives the impression of being too heavy. Other fine *phiale* are at Dochiariou and Koutloumoussiou.

TOWERS

Practically every monastery still has its fortified tower, and from an architectural point of view the towers are generally the most pleasing feature of the entire group of buildings. They are built according to two different schemes. But there is no chronological relation between the two forms, and merely from looking at it, it would be hardly possible to tell at what period a tower was built.

The first type of tower is the simple square block, crenellated, but without machicolations. The earliest and finest of all is at Lavra, built in 970 by the Emperor Tzimiskes. It is low and squat, with small well-set windows, and gives a magnificent impression of strength through its massive proportions. Later towers of this kind are to be found at Pantokrator (fourteenth century?), Dionysiou (1520) and St Paul's (1522).* A certain tendency for the tower to develop in height is visible, so that the tower of St Paul's is quite tall and narrow.

The other towers are crenellated, but also machicolated. That of Chilandari (possibly 1190) is among the earliest.† The most important date, however, from the sixteenth century: Karakallou (early sixteenth century) and Dochiariou (1520) have particularly successful examples, with very fine proportions. Stavronikita, too, has a good tower from this period (1540).

BELFRY TOWERS

Although bells are very little used on Mount Athos, a number of

---

* Koutloumoussiou might be added (1508).
† Also ruined tower of Amalfitans (thirteenth century), and tower of Milutin (1302?)

monasteries have belfry towers. Some stand quite free, some are attached to the church, while others are set in the buildings surrounding the court. The best date from the eighteenth century, though one or two are earlier (Vatopèdi 1427, Iviron 1513). They almost all have pointed roofs, with small projecting gables on each side; and consist of a series of stories of double arches, the lower of which are usually closed. The belfries of Gregoriou (1776), Karyes (1781), St Anne's (1784) and Xiropotamou (1779) closely follow this type. They are all built in the typical eighteenth-century manner, with alternating bands of stone and brick.

Dionysiou has a peculiar step-gabled dovecote and an Italianate belfry, unique on Athos, but common on the islands, while St Pantaleïmon has an elaborate octagonal belfry (early nineteenth century).

APPENDIX VII

Dates of Buildings on Mount Athos[1]

KARYES

10th c. (middle)	Church of Protàton, rebuilt in 1508.
	Paintings traditionally *c.* 1300, probably early 16th *c.*
1781	Bell tower.

KOUTLOUMOUSSIOU

1508	Tower (Smyrnakes,[2] p. 523).
16th c. (early)	Church.
	North chapel, 1733.
	Exo-narthex, 1744.
1767	East range (Smyrnakes, p. 523).
1808	Bell tower (Hasluck).
1860–97	New buildings.

IVIRON

1492–1513	Main period of rebuilding of church.
	Floor, 976; small columns with carved capitals, 976.
	Iconostasis, 1614.
	Exo-narthex repaired, 1614.
1513	Clock tower (Millet,[3] 220).
1625	Arsenal (Millet, 289, 290).
1680–83	Chapel of Portaïtissa (Millet, 263–4).
1848	Refectory (Millet, 275).
1860–85	New buildings; porch of entrance.

STAVRONIKITA

16th c.	Tower.
1546–53–1628	Church (Millet, 201–3).
1770	Refectory (Millet, 211).
1810	Synodikon (Millet, 213).

---

1 Most of the information in this appendix is taken from Hasluck, *Athos and Its Monasteries*.
2 Smyrnakes, 'The Holy Mountain'.
3 *Recueil des Inscriptions Chrétiennes du Mont Athos,* i.

PANTOKRATOR

14th c. (?)   Tower.
1363   Church.
                   Altered and restored in 1847 and 1854 (narthex rebuilt).
1536   Walls (Millet, 161).
18th c.   All the existing buildings except tower and church.

VATOPEDI

14th c. (beginning)   Main period of reconstruction of church, originally built in the end of the 10th c.
                   Paintings in church 1312 (restored at a later period). Mosaics over central doorway in exo-narthex 14th c.
1427   Bell tower.
1785   Refectory.
1794   Chapel of Zone.

ESPHIGMENOU

1716   Parts of west range (Smyrnakes, p. 640).
1808–11   Church (Smyrnakes, p. 641).
1810   Refectory (Smyrnakes, p. 647).
1854–58   New buildings (Smyrnakes p. 640).

CHILANDARI

12th c.(?)   Tower (restored 1688) (Smyrnakes, p. 485).
1293   Church.
                   Pavement, c. 1197.
                   Exo-narthex, 1374.
1302(?)   Tower of Milutin between monastery and sea.
18th c. (late)   West range near church, south range, and refectory.
19th c. (early)   North part of west range.

ZOGRAPHOU

1764   Old church (Smyrnakes, p. 558).
1801   New church (Smyrnakes p. 557).
1810   Clock tower (Smyrnakes, p. 558).
19th c. (early)   Eastern range.
1860–96   New buildings.

KASTAMONITOU

1828   North part of east range (Smyrnakes, p. 685).
1820   S.E. corner with arcades.
1867   Church.
1885   Part of east range (Smyrnakes, p. 685).

DOCHIARIOU

16th c.	Tower. Restored in 1617 (Smyrnakes, p. 571).
1547	Refectory (Smyrnakes, p 570).
1568	Church with frescoes.
	North chapel, 1636 (Smyrnakes, p. 569).
1704	Bell tower.
1753	Guest house (Hasluck).
1768–83	Iconostasis in main church (Brockhaus,[4] p. 293, no. 139)

XENOPHONTOS

16th c. (middle)	Refectory.
	Paintings in refectory 17th c. (Brockhaus, p. 293, no. 133).
	Old church.
	Pavement 11th c. (Brockhaus, p. 288, no. 20).
	Mosaics of St George and St Demetrius, 14th c.
	Paintings, middle of 16th c.
1800	Seaward range (Hunt in Walpole's *Memoirs*, p. 216).
1817–37	New church (Brockhaus, p. 294, no. 150).

ST PANTALEIMON

1812–14	Old building (Brockhaus, p. 294, no. 146).
1812–21	Main church in courtyard (Smyrnakes, 666).
1892	Refectory.
1808	Large church on top floor of north wing.

XIROPOTAMOU

1763	Church (Millet, 571; Smyrnakes, p. 546).
1779	Clock tower (Millet, p. 558).
1780–81	Building S.E. of clock tower (Millet, p. 564).
1779–1820	South range (Millet, p. 565).
1819	South-east angle (Millet, p. 569).

SIMOPETRA

1567	Arsenal (Millet, p. 536).
1891	Monastery destroyed by fire.
1891–1902	Monastery entirely rebuilt on old foundations.
1893	Church

GREGORIOU

1761	Monastery destroyed by fire (Millet, p. 496).
c. 1776	Cells to north (Millet, p. 515).
1779	Paintings of church (Millet, p. 515).
1783	Cells to south (Millet, p. 514).
1891–1900	New buildings.

[4] *Die Kunst in dem Athos-Klöstern.*

DIONYSIOU

1520	Tower (Millet, p. 494).
1577	Church and frescoes (Millet, p. 458).
16th c.	Refectory.
	Paintings, 1603 (Millet, p. 491).

ST PAUL'S

1522	Tower (Millet, pp. 446–7).
1844	Church (Millet, pp. 428–9).
After 1902	Present buildings except tower and a small frescoed chapel dedicated to St George.

LAVRA

970	'Tower of Tzimiskes' repaired in 1522, 1564, 1688 (Millet, pp. 411–41).
Before 16th c.	Main church.
	Traditionally built in 963 by St Athanasius, founder of the monastery.
	Narthex rebuilt 1814.
	Paintings, 1535 (Millet, p. 339).
	Paintings of Chapel of St Nicholas, 1560 (Millet, p. 373).
	Paintings of Chapel of Forty Martyrs, 1578 (Millet, p. 369).
1512	Refectory finished.
16th c.	Part of southern range.
16th c.	Phiale.
1643–53	Chapel of St Michael of Synnada (Millet, p. 383).
1713	Chapel of Panagia Koukouzelítissa (Millet, p. 377; Smyrnakes, p. 390).
1769	South east range.
18th c. (end)	Guest-house. Originally built 1580 (Millet, p. 388).

KARAKALLOU

16th c.	Tower.
1707	Cells to north (Millet, p. 325).
1714	Church rebuilt (Millet, pp. 306–7).
1879	Refectory (Millet, p. 323).
1880	Fire and partial rebuilding of E. wing (Smyrnakes, p. 578).

PHILOTHEOU

| 1747–65 | Church and paintings (Millet, p. 292, and Smyrnakes, p. 584). |
| After 1871 | Buildings of court (Smyrnakes, p. 585). |

Glossary

There are two types of monastery on Athos:
(1) 'coenobian', the basis of which is communistic.
(2) 'idiorhythmic', in which the monks are allowed to possess
property.

Skite	Organised group of small houses round church.
Kellion	Detached cottage with one or more cells.
Phiale	Sacred well.
Symandron	Wooden gong for announcing services.
Epitrope	Member of the Administrative Council (of an idiorhythmic monastery).
Ierondas	Equivalent to Russian 'Starez': usually the master of a group of novices. Also used as a polite form of address to any elderly monk.

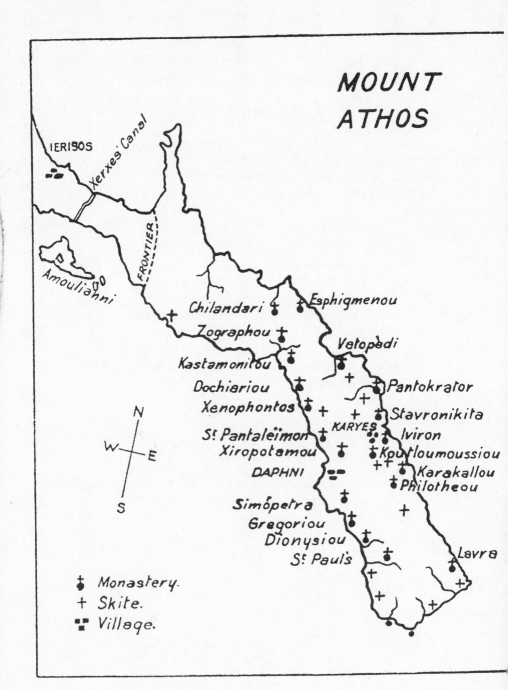

MOUNT
ATHOS

IERISOS

Xerxes Canal

FRONTIER

Amouliahni

Chilandari   Esphigmenou

Zographou

Kastamonitou   Vatopedi

Dochiariou   Pantokrator
Xenophontos
                          Stavronikita
                    KARYES
St. Pantaleïmon   Iviron
Xiropotamou   Koutloumoussiou
                                Karakallou
DAPHNI   Philotheou

Simópetra
Gregoriou
Dionysiou
St. Paul's   Lavra

N
W   E
S

♰ Monastery.
✝ Skite.
☗ Village.